Life Injections IV

Still More Connections of Scripture to the Human Experience

Richard E. Zajac

Parson's Porch Books

Life Injections IV: Still More Connections of Scripture to the Human Experience

ISBN: Softcover 978-0692424650

Copyright © 2015 by Richard E. Zajac

All rights reserved. No part of this book may be reproduced or transmitted in any form or by any means, electronic or mechanical, including photocopying, recording, or by any information storage and retrieval system, without permission in writing from the publisher.

To order additional copies of this book, contact:

Parson's Porch Books

1-423-475-7308

www.parsonsporch.com

Parson's Porch Books is an imprint of Parson's Porch & Company (PP&C) in Cleveland, Tennessee. PP&C is an innovative non-profit organization which raises money by publishing books of noted authors, representing all genres. All donations from contributors and profits from publishing are shared with the poor.

To My Brother Bob and My Sister In Law Ginny
Who Keep Me Grounded and Humble

Advance Praise for Life Injections IV

This is Father Zajac's fourth book in a series called "Life Injections," and it is clear, that he has not run out of insights. It is amazing that Father Zajac continues to find in the simplest of daily interactions and observations, 'injections' as he calls them, that ultimately lead one to dwell on the more profound aspects of life. But Father Zajac's real gift is the ability to link, to link the ordinary with the extraordinary and then to remind us that this is indeed one of life's most important tasks. Reading these vignettes will help you see how to make that link and it is that connection which will ultimately serve to deepen your own spirituality.

I imagine Father Zajac to be a kind of gyroscope with antennae sticking out all over the place. The antennae are constantly searching and capturing the quotidian, the mundane, the commonplace and then, as only Father Zajac can do it, to metamorphose these into something deeper, richer and certainly, more fulfilling. For sure this is a gift, at once simple and profound. And is this not what a spiritual journal is all about, viz., taking the ordinary and lifting it to a higher plane? You will find in reading this book that your own perspective on life will change, some changes will be dramatic, some almost imperceptible, but in either case, the changes will lead you to a richer and more fulfilling life.

Peter Markulis, Ph.D.
Professor of Management
State University of New York at Geneseo

Today's Christian preachers face unique challenges. The task of presenting an ancient deposit of faith, framed in terms and concepts which are obscure to a secularized society in the Postmodern Era, is indeed a daunting task. Catholic preachers in particular, because of the nature of our worship, have less time to make their points, making every homiletic occasion exceedingly valuable and not time to be squandered.

In Life Injections IV, *a collection of his homilies, Father Richard Zajac's words break out of the small confines of the Chapel at Sisters Hospital in Buffalo, New York, to a much wider audience, effectively declaring the Gospel in our times.*

Blessed with exceptional wordsmithing and linguistic skills, Father "Duke" uses a style similar to Jesus's own midrashic teaching method, employing multiple examples from history, literature and current culture to support a particular theme taken from the Scripture reading of the day. Most importantly, Life Injections IV *addresses common human issues faced by the Christian faithful on a regular basis, such as gossip, depression, our physical mortality, anger, disillusionment and a multitude of similar traits of the human condition.*

Using a variety of rhetorical techniques ranging from humor to poignancy, Father Zajac delivers messages that demand appropriate responses from his readers. His ministry expands from the patients and staff at Sisters Hospital to a more extensive patient base which is all of us who are in need of spiritual healing and growth.

Charles B. McVeigh, M.P.H., M.A., FACHE
Principal, Pilot Healthcare Group, Aurora, Ohio

Father Duke Zajac has hit a homerun with the publication of the fourth volume of Life Injections. *In his own inimitable way, he has blended the wisdom of his hospital experience with the good news of the Gospels and created a prescription that can heal the weary soul of almost any 21st century Christian. If you need a shot in the arm, some solid advice or just a great story to lift your spirits, you are sure to find it in* Life Injections IV.

Rev. Dr. Robert J. Perelli CJM
Founder, The Center for Family Systems Theory, Inc.

Father Zajac's reflective, thoughtful sermons allow all who read this treasure the opportunity to realize how God is present to us in the ordinary, in the everyday experiences of life. They provide a framework of support, encouragement and awe as we marvel at the many ways God is with us on the journey. The Scripture passages identified and related sermons call each of us to contemplative, reflective moments of self-awareness and inner peace.

Paula Moscato
Vice President Mission Integration
Sisters of Charity Hospital, Buffalo, New York

In a world that often provides little comfort or meaning, and in a culture that idealizes quick fixes, Father Zajac provides both comfort and meaning by interweaving words of the Gospel with masterful storytelling and poignant personal anecdotes. Father Zajac invites us to marvel at nature, and at fellow humans who reveal God's love. He reminds us that to benefit from our experiences, even suffering, we must allow ourselves the time to learn from it. Sometimes we cannot find the words to adequately capture our human experience. We need stories for that. In Life Injections IV, *that is exactly how Father Zajac touches our inner lives.*

Dr. Jim Butters
Licensed Psychologist with East Amherst Psychology Group, LLP
Buffalo, New York

In Life Injections IV, *Father Zajac once again brings the Scripture message into the age and place in which we live today. These 26 presentations, several of which I was fortunate enough to have heard delivered, raise our awareness of the timeliness of the Bible as we deal with our daily lives. I add this to the previous volumes and will revisit it as I do the earlier publications.*

Sister Mary Anne Brawley
Board Chair Emeritus
Our Lady of Lourdes Memorial Hospital, Binghamton, New York

Praise for Life Injections III

Father Zajac's compassion, wisdom, love of God and life is expressed through sermons with timeless messages that has meaning and value for all people. This is a book that could and should be read and reread many times and always used as a source of comfort, self-awareness, and enlightenment.

Lana D. Benatovich
President, The National Federation for Just Communities

Father Zajac's Life Injections III *takes Scripture and relates it to stories of everyday life which get the reader to reflect on their own feelings, thoughts and experiences. Each chapter was applicable to something I have thought or felt at one time or another in my life. The great thing about the book is not only is it a great resource for those who give homilies, but it is a greater resource for those who read them. A must-read for all walks of life.*

Mark Simon
President/CEO, Upstate New York Transplant Services

Father Zajac's introduction defends his belief that even brevity can be excessive--a paradox perhaps but a verity demonstrated throughout his sermons. Recalling Pascal's famous apology for the long letter he hadn't the time to make short, Zajac strikes the Goldilocks mean. The test is the grip of the stories, offered with rich anecdote and allusion to bring the message of the gospel to the experience of everyday and everyone's life. If you haven't heard them spoken, you will emerge from the reading refreshed, hopeful, and a lot wiser.

Ray Bissonette, PhD
Associate Professor of Family Medicine, University of Buffalo (emeritus)

This book of sermons is thoughtful and spiritually provocative. Father Zajac is a talented preacher whose research, insights and skillful storytelling enliven lessons from the New Testament with tales from life's journey to expose the unlimited wisdom and application of Scripture in our everyday actions and interactions. Each chapter contains lessons to soften the heart, strengthen the will and heal the soul. Read One-A-Day to live an extraordinary life, read two or more when you waver from that path.

Lucille Sherlick PhD
Family Special Projects and EAP Liaison
Community Missions, Niagara Falls, NY

In Life Injections III, *Father Richard Zajac provides the reader with 28 sermons/stories that vibrantly resonate with invaluable lessons concerning the human experience. Characters in his tales range from Rabbi Harold Kushner to St. Teresa to Popeye. Father Zajac weaves tales from the simplest of items-a cookie jar-to something as profound as the voice of God.* Life Injections III *yields an exciting, all inspiring and impeccably practical treatise on thoughtful and purposeful living.*

William Zorn, PhD
Director of Family Services
SUNY Buffalo

Using numerous inspirational, insightful, uplifting, thought-provoking, oftentimes humorous stories, Father Zajac challenges complacency, decries negativism, encourages flexibility, emphasizes involvement and the importance of being grateful for our gifts and fulfilling the plan for which they were given. He shows how ordinary lives can become no less than extraordinary if one is willing to go the extra step. Life Injections III *is an excellent resource book for ministers preparing purposeful, meaningful homilies. Concomitantly, the faithful will find this book filled with refreshing, relevant and practical applications of Scripture to daily life. It's a refreshing, easy read, hard to put down, great for meditation, a perfect gift!*

Rose Domondon
Lay Minister
Our Lady of Good Counsel Church
Pearl City, Hawaii

Father Zajac as a hospital chaplain, who is an entertaining writer and an exceptionally keen observer of life. His writings reflect the wisdom, intelligence, insight, humor and spiritual strength of someone who loves life and the people in it. In this book, he has gifted us with 29 cleverly developed homilies relating Scripture to his experiences and his enjoyment of sports, travel, history and politics, art and literature, movies and cartoons, illness and healing, ministry and church, people and the full range of human emotions within life! What an inspiration it was to read! And what a wonderful gift this would be for the religious and clergy in our lives as well as for anyone who just wants a commonsense connection to Scripture.

Barbara Kozeliski
Director of Religious Education (emeritus)
Gallup, New Mexico

I love Father Zajac's books. They are uplifting and inspirational. I'm delighted that Volume III is being published. It's the kind of book you want to have on hand when you need your spiritual batteries recharged.

Lorene Hanley Duquin
Director of Family Life
St. John the Baptist Church
Lockport, NY

Father Zajac's homilies helped me to listen to the Word more attentively; his practical expressions modeled ways to live that word, especially helping me to examine my life from "what I have done" and, as importantly, "what I have not done." Father Zajac has forced me to connect our faith to my everyday life in a world that often wants to be disconnected. His stories, jokes, literary footnotes and connections to popular culture, helped me to see how the word is truly incarnated in simple experiences.

Brian Corbin
Executive Director of Catholic Charities
Youngstown, NY

Father Zajac's compassion and understanding of the human condition on many levels is portrayed in this magnificent book. It meets us in the reality and trenches of life applying humor and wisdom that not only enters into our universal human experience, but draws scripture into the 21st century. You'll find eye-opening, teachable moments and generous insights as he shares his own experiences and observations of human frailties and ironies. He's a brilliant talent and gift! As I have personally known Duke to be a person of integrity, humility and truly authentic; you too will know him in this way as you read each segment. I've used previous books in Spirituality groups, sermons and for personal reflection and I'm grateful to be able to add another to my collection.

Carol Mazurek
Director of Spiritual Care (emeritus)
St. Mary's Medical Center
Huntington, West Virginia

Praise for Life Injections II

The fruits of years of experience as a hospital chaplain, Zajac diagrams clearly the most difficult of daily life problems avoiding the slightest clichés of pop theology and taking the reader to a newer place of freedom. I can't help thinking it's the book to give someone whose life is off the track for any reason. More than homilies, they are reflections on the Scriptures, meditations for everyone to start or close the day, tools for not just getting by but getting better. From forgiveness to prejudices, gutsy questions about justice, envy, boredom and burnout, gratitude, fatigue, rejection, false piety, pretense, lack of virtue, self-pity; he manages to cover the gamut most of us will feel at one time every day of our lives and invites us to drag ourselves out into a newer world. By the all too often unaware, he slowly but strongly builds a quilt of powerful stories tightly sewn and not easily forgotten. You'll shed some tears, you'll smile gently or even laugh somewhere in each chapter and at the end of everyone you will say "Wow!" You'll want to write your Congressman, to pray more, to do more, to love more, to be more. Life Injections II is simply wonderful. Give all your friends a copy!

Rev. Msgr. J. Patrick Keleher
Director of Catholic Campus Ministry
State University of New York at Buffalo

Once again, Father Zajac taps into the fundamental need of the human heart for a good story. Whether we seek new light on a dilemma we face, consolation or comfort in distress, a bit of challenge in a time of routine, or the simple reassurance that we're not walking the human pathway alone; there is sustenance to be found here for our inner life. Father Zajac himself has listened well to the stories of God's way of being with us, told in the Scriptures and in the events and experiences of life.

Sister Maureen McGuire
Vice President/ Service Culture Development
Catholic Health Care System, Buffalo, New York

Father Zajac's stories make it easy for the "saints" who sit around the kitchen table every day working, planning and providing for their families to apply the Christian ideal to their lives. The rich variety of tales including Aesop's fables, the wise Rabbi stories, modern sports anecdotes, and the movies, the footnotes of history, the song lyrics, and the novels keep the reader not only interested but challenged by giving a fresh and creative perspective on the gospel stories they have heard all their lives.

Deacon Lee Pico
St. Mary's Cathedral
Cheyenne, Wyoming

Once again, in his new book, Father Zajac has found a way to turn simple stories into profound truths. In unearthing these universal messages and bringing them to light, he draws us closer to God and to each other.

Paula Voell
Reporter
Buffalo News

The title of the book accurately describes the context for the reader in that scenes from human life are injected into a biblical text with the result that one comes away with a refreshed insight into God's activity in the real world. The reader will gain a fresh and challenging perspective on living one's life in accord with the living Word of God. The experienced preacher who may be seeking to improve his/her craft, the aspiring preacher who may be struggling to find an appropriate example, or the person in the pew who is looking for a deeper appreciation of the Scriptures, will all benefit from this book.

Rev. Kevin Mullen, OFM, PhD
St. Leo's Church
Elmwood Park, New Jersey

At the start of the third millennium, Father Zajac offers a view of life and love that is real. It's not glamorized by the more, the glitzy or the extravagant. Rather, it's an unpretentious awareness of the magnificence of ordinary human experience. The key to appreciating Life Injections II *is to love life with its characteristic ups and downs yet always believing in the transformative power of the Word of God. Zajac does it and it shows. Anyone struggling with the vicissitudes of the human experience will be challenged to view life differently and face it head-on. It's a great little book to guide us in an unabashed look at ourselves through the trials and triumphs of others. What a great tool to motivate us to live and love more genuinely.*

Sister Anne Marie Jablonicky, CSSF
Psychologist and Counselor
Diocesan Counseling Center
Buffalo, New York

Father Zajac's second book of Life Injections *gave me as much enjoyment and food for thought as the first one. I found something that spoke directly to my daily experiences. Father Zajac has a wonderful way of connecting Scripture to everyday life, weaving great stories in to help carry out his message. The book is a great resource for homilies as well as for personal reflection.*

Julie French
Lay Preacher and Lay Presider
Scobey, Montana

Praise for Life Injections I

George Burns once said: "a sermon should have a good beginning, a good ending and hopefully they are close together." We can be grateful Father Zajac does not subscribe to this philosophy! Not only do his beginnings and endings claim our attention, so too is most of what is in between food for the journey. The sermons Father Zajac has shared with us reveal the soul of a man who is not only well read but also well lived in the joys and sorrows and foibles of the human predicament. There is not a sermon in this collection where he does not tie his thoughts together with actual experience. To use one of his own illustrations: Father Zajac has closed the gap between his head and his heart and given us a group of sermons that ring true. In reading many of them, I felt he was holding a mirror up to my face; I strongly suspect this is one of the greatest gifts he has to share.

Rev. Cynthia Bronson Sweigert
The Church of the Redeemer (Episcopal)
Pittsburgh, Pennsylvania

The "Good News" simply put in concrete vocabulary, without losing Christ's true message!

Sister Marie Burns
Chairperson of the Board
Sisters Hospital of Buffalo and St. Mary's Hospital of Rochester

A little spark can light a mighty flame. There is not a sermon here of Father Zajac's that does not abound in sparks that will turn his readers to caring afresh for our muddled, hope filled human family, and connecting Scripture to our human experience.

Rev. Ross Mackenzie
Director of Religion
Chautauqua Institution

Richard Zajac addresses important Christian life situations with engaging, reflective, down to earth illustrations sourced in selective scriptural texts. Each of his 22 sermonic explorations invite the reader to consider how the Christian message injects life. For personal meditation or public proclamation, these well drawn talks developed somewhat in "Christopher Notes" style offer a wealth of traditional and new insights on important human questions. Zajac laces his presentations with humor and practical wisdom inviting the reader to adopt and absorb the message into their own lives. At times entertaining, often challenging, easy-to-read, always interest holding, this is an excellent collection of scriptural-based, practically applied, deeply Christian talks.

Rev. Paul Steller
Catholic Campus Minister
Erie Community College, North Campus

Father Zajac's book is in the best tradition of storytelling. It is also in the best tradition of Christian preaching that dates back to the Nazarene preacher. Through the centuries, Jesus has held our attention with the story of the father waiting to forgive and take home his wayward son and the story of the stranger who rescues the mugging victim ignored by the passerby. This collection of sermons is an interesting fast read. Have your pencil ready to mark off the stories you especially like and wish to make use of yourself.

Rev. John Mergenhagen
Retreat Director
Author of Audio Cassette Series: *Eye of the Heart* and *Freeing the Christ Within*

Reading Life Injections is like reading a book of short stories each with its small cast of characters facing life's dilemmas which somehow don't seem as complicated under the glow of Father Zajac's insight. Life Injections is a collage of fables a modern Aesop might write revealing that though life is indeed difficult, it is not necessarily complicated. Like most great preachers, Father Zajac uses poignant and often humorous parables of everyday life to animate simple truths that bring serenity to the troubled and wisdom to those who are searching. If Paul were writing his apostles in 1998 instead of 0056, he would be hard-pressed to *convey more insights than flaws from Father Zajac's entrancing "stories" of general truths that bring simple answers to the dilemmas of our human condition.*

Thomas T. Frantz PhD
Chair of Department of Counseling and Education Psychology
SUNY Buffalo

Table of Contents

Introduction	21
Loosening Up	23
Depression	29
Marveling	36
What You Heard Said	42
Saying No	48
Quality of Friendships	53
The Morphing of Peace	59
Attention Deficit Disorder	65
Excellence	71
Imperfection	77
Inclusive not Exclusive	83
Life Expectancy	88
The Invitation to Live	94
Nothing Matters	98
Surprise	104
Is There any Hope	110
Remember Not the Things of the Past	116
Being a Somebody	121
The 24/7 Mentality	127
Loneliness	133
Saying Nice Things	139
Essentials	145
Siamese Twins	151
Hiss but Do Not Bite	156

Watchmen and Watchwomen	162
If Disillusionment Comes Your Way	168
Just Do It	174
Amplius	180
Endnotes	186

Introduction

I've been in hospital ministry for over thirty two years and a regular part of that ministry involves wake-up calls in the middle of the night, often to minister to families who have lost a loved one, sometimes to bless a baby too tiny to live, and frequently to broker an emergency where a decision needs to be made in regards to life supportive measures being administered to an elderly parent who had just taken ill. Since our hospital is not a trauma center, I am usually spared some of the more horrendous hospital emergencies but that's not to say that there have not been times when a night call has taxed every ounce of my ministerial ability. And many were the occasion where that ministry resulted in the forfeiture of a full night's sleep.

I've shared with you this information because some of the sermons which grace this book were born as a result of my middle of the night ministry. Early on, I found that hitting the pillow upon my return to bed never resulted in sleep. I was a bit too "wired" for that to happen. Thus began my regiment of reading sermons to "decompress", my perusing the collected works of some of the great preachers of the past and present to ready my mind and body for the sleep it yearned to receive.

I first began reading the books of Harry Emerson Fosdick whom I believe is the best preacher of the previous century and I followed his seven books of sermons with the twenty or odd volumes of essays by the Australian preacher F.W. Boreham, essays that were in fact his weekly message to the congregations he served. Some of my most interesting illustrations have been lifted from those essays. The works of Boreham were followed by those of J. Wallace Hamilton, a Methodist pastor from Florida, and then the three books of the famous Peter Marshall who served as chaplain to the United States Congress back in the 50's. Most recently I completed the two-volume set of sermons by the late William Sloane Coffin and a few months back I was graced by Episcopalian Samuel T. Lloyd III whose book captured his best efforts to break apart the Word of God for the congregation of the National Cathedral in

Washington D.C. I'm presently reading the work of the Baptist Otis Moss III whom I believe is the best preacher of our time.

As I may have alluded to in a previous volume, on the back page of each of the books of sermons I have completed, I'll note the page of an illustration which needs to be copied as well as the page of a sermon(s) where I thought the author cleverly worked the Scripture passage upon which it was based. The latter notation will then be inscribed in the margin of the Sunday Lectionary where that passage happens to be found. Given the volume of sermons I have read, I may have as many as a dozen inscriptions for one particular Sunday and, should I have to preach that day, I'll re-read those noted sermons hoping for an angle of vision or a topic upon which I can direct my thoughts.

I've never stolen or plagiarized someone else's work but I've never been averse to using their idea and making it my own. Many of the sermons you're about to read may well have come to life thanks to a great preacher whose sermon helped ready me for the pillow I had left when my phone rang in the middle of the night.

Loosening Up

Mark 7: 31-37

"...He said 'Ephphatha!', that is 'Be opened!...'"

There's joy to be had when parts of us get loosed.

I've heard recently of an Episcopal Church where a newly appointed Deacon had been put in charge of preparing the elements for communion. At the start of the service, the pastor happened to notice that the wine looked particularly dark but he never gave it a second thought. When it came time for communion, the pastor as well as the congregation shockingly discovered the reason for the wine's darkness. The deacon had mistakenly substituted prune juice for the wine. After the service, one of the congregants made an astute observation. He said: "Maybe the prune juice wasn't a mistake. Maybe it was God trying to tell us that we need a little loosening up."

Well, it's loosening up I'd like to talk with you about today. More specifically, it's opening up I'd like to discuss with you today. Jesus in our Gospel opens up a man's ear and loosens up the same man's tongue and all rejoiced. My contention is that if certain parts of us get opened up and loosened up, all will rejoice as well.

Let's take our pocketbooks for starters. I love the story of the gentleman who was given a tour of the Mann Center for the Performing Arts in Tel Aviv, Israel. The tour guide was pointing out the features of the incredible structure. The stoneware was unbelievably beautiful. The wall tapestries, the paintings, the gold inlays were absolutely marvelous. Finally, the tourist said: "I assume you named the facility for Horace Mann, the famous author?" And the tour guide answered with a smile: "No! We named it for Frederick Mann of Philadelphia." The tourist remarked: "Frederick

Mann? What did he write?" And the tour guide answered: "He wrote a check."

Many a wonderful art gallery, many a beautiful park, many a tremendous organization and many a phenomenal human service agency have come into being thanks to checks written by generous people. Thanks to the willingness of many people to open up and loosen up their pocketbooks.

I've always liked that story of a bag of old money about to be shredded. As time passed, the $20 bill and a $1 bill inside the bag got into a conversation. The $20 bill regaled the dollar bill with all of his exploits. He told of his leading an exciting life: casinos, resorts, grand hotels, cruises. The dollar bill just shook his head and complained as to how he led a boring life. "Week after week," he said, "it was the same old thing: church, church, church!"

If we're going to get the entire world to rejoice, then the opening and the loosening of our pocketbooks needs to center not upon ourselves, not upon resorts or casinos or cruises; it needs to center on church related activities. It needs to center on worthwhile causes, people in need and organizations put together for the betterment of humankind. When that kind of opening up and loosening up of our pocketbooks takes place, a lot of good happens and the entire world does rejoice.

Then there's the matter of the opening and the loosening of our mouths. There's a story about a twelve year old boy who in all of his twelve years had never spoken a word. After being served oatmeal for breakfast several days in a row, a miracle happened. To everyone's shock, he spoke. He said: "Yuk! I hate oatmeal!" The family was aghast and beside themselves with joy. The mother ran across the room and threw her arms around her son's neck and cried: "For 12 long years, your father and I were convinced you couldn't talk. How is it that you never spoke a word to us before?" Very bluntly, the boy explained: "Well, mom, up until now everything was all right!"

That funny story relates to a truth, that truth being that we usually do keep quiet when everything's all right with us. We hold our tongues when all is well with us. And the only time when we seem to break away from that pattern is when all is not right, when all is not well with us. We speak, we open our mouths when some inconvenience or an injustice or some bad thing intrudes upon our life. In the meantime, there are all sorts of important issues in need of a voice. There are needy and desperate people in need of words of support. There are all sorts of bad things in need of a cry of protest. All kinds of misbehavior in need of a shout of disgust. And unfortunately, all too often, we don't say a word. Not a sound emerges from our mouths.

For all the world to rejoice at the opening of and the loosening of our mouths, then that opening and that loosening needs to center not upon our problems and troubles, but upon the problems and troubles of others especially those less fortunate than we are. It needs to come from a genuine anger and a real upset over the injustices and the cruelties which happen to get heaped upon them.

Civil Rights leader Martin Luther King Jr. said that in the end we will remember not the words of our enemy; instead we will remember the silence of our friends. So we need to open up and loosen up our mouths so it will never be said of us that we were a silent friend, that it will never be said that we spoke not a word when some evil unfolded before us.

And then you have the matter of the opening up and the loosening up of our ears. There's a little shop in Spokane Washington on an out of the way street where for $15 you can talk to somebody for a half an hour, someone who promises to listen to you without interruption and without offering advice. It's staffed by laypeople and it's called "Let's Talk." People pay that $15 gladly and consider it a bargain because they've come to discover that good listeners are hard to find.

There are all sorts of people in this world yearning to pour out their souls, yearning to spill their guts, yearning to unload a burden deep inside them and, quite sadly, there really aren't many willing to loosen and open their ears to hear them, not many who will sit down so their anguish and their pain could be heard.

I recall a colleague, the Rev. Mark Gregory, a Methodist minister, who lives in Allegheny County Virginia. A few years ago he lost his wife and not long after he lost two of his children. He was telling of how bad a time that proved to be especially following their funerals. But then he told of a dear lady who dropped by one day, sat down in his home, and simply said: "I am here to listen!" Moments later he broke down and poured out his soul to that woman.

Most of us hear very well but unfortunately we're not very good at listening. For all to rejoice at the opening and the loosening of our ears, it's going to take more than just allowing words to enter the cavity of our ear. It'll take genuine listening. It'll take being absorbed in what others are trying to tell us. It's the kind of listening the people in Spokane Washington are paying for at $15 a half an hour.

And then there's the matter of the opening and the loosening of our eyes. A Rabbi was giving instructions to some children when he posed this question: "How do you know the night is over and the day has come?" Puzzled, the children took time to answer. One of them said: "You know the night is over and the day has come when at dawn you look out at a tree and you can tell whether it's an apple or a pear tree. The Rabbi acknowledged the response but repeated the question. A second student said: "You know that night is over and the day has come when you see an animal in the distance and you can tell whether it's a donkey or a horse. The Rabbi acknowledged his response but then repeated the question again. By this time, the students were too puzzled and exasperated to come up with a response. So they asked the Rabbi to answer the question. The Rabbi said: "You know that the night is over and the day has come when you look in the eyes of any human being and you see there your brother or your sister. For if you do not see your brother or sister, it is still night."

If we open up and loosen up our eyes and see as that Rabbi suggests, all will rejoice because it will mean that we're color blind. We won't discriminate because of the color of one's skin. If we open up and loosen up our eyes and see as that Rabbi suggests, all will rejoice because we won't overlook the street person or the poor person. We won't fail to see that one who talks funny or the one who looks funny or the one everyone seems to be ignoring. If more of us could start seeing as the Rabbi suggests, all will rejoice because it will be the end of prejudice, the end of apathy and bigotry.

So there is the opening and the loosening of our pocketbooks, our ears, our mouths, our eyes, and then there's the opening up and the loosening up of our minds. In Edgar Allen Poe's haunting story *The Cask of Amontillado*[1], he tells of the revenge taken by a man against an enemy. That enemy was invited down into the wine cellar and told to step into a narrow circular shaped closet and select a bottle of fine wine. When he stepped inside, the opening was immediately sealed off and the man left there to die.

Many a person unconsciously gives that same brutal treatment to their mind. They allow their minds to be hemmed in by old thoughts and old ideas and old thinking and old ways of doing things, shutting out all that's new and different and fresh. And unfortunately, as was the fate of that man in that closet, a mind so sealed will eventually die.

There are all of these exciting new ideas, all of these new ways of looking at life, all of this new information being processed every day. And if we open our minds to it, if we loosen up our thinking and take it all in, all will rejoice because less will be mistaken notions, less will be erroneous beliefs, and misunderstandings will finally be seen for what they are.

And then finally, there is the matter of the opening up and loosening up of our wills. In the Star Wars movie: *The Empire Strikes Back*, Luke Skywalker flies his X-Way Plane to a swamp planet to seek and find a Jedi Master named Yoda to teach him the ways of becoming a Jedi warrior so he can free the galaxy of the evil tyrant Darth Vader. Yoda reluctantly agrees and begins by teaching him how to lift rocks with his mental powers. One day, Yoda tells Luke to lift his spaceship from the swamp with his mind. Luke complains that lifting rocks is one thing but lifting a spaceship is quite another. Yoda insists and Luke gives it a try and fails. Yoda then focuses his mind and soon thereafter the spaceship arises from the murky waters. Luke, with his mouth open, exclaims: "I don't believe it!" Yoda looks at him and says: "That's why you couldn't lift it. You didn't believe you could!"

Opening up and loosening up our wills means being bound and determined to make something happen despite what skeptics have to say, despite the word impossible attached to its accomplishment.

If done, all will rejoice because it will have made a dream come true.

In our Gospel today, Jesus opens up a man's ears and loosens up a man's tongue and all were astonished and all rejoiced. We pray that the Lord will open up and loosen up our pocketbooks and our ears and our mouths and our minds and our wills. Our pocketbooks, so we may provide the capital so some worthwhile project or service may find the light of day. Our ears, so we will listen to some wounded soul. Our mouths, so some good cause will have a voice. Our eyes, so we can see the homeless man as our brother and the bag lady as our sister. Our minds, so negative and false thinking may be no more. Our wills, so some impossible dream may come true. If all of that happens, the entire world will indeed rejoice.

Depression

Job 7: 1-4, 6-7

"...Is not one's life on earth a drudgery?..."

What we are to do and what we are to make of depression

Joseph Grimaldi is remembered as history's greatest clown. He lived at the beginning of the 19th century and entertained amongst others the King of England. He was hailed as a man who could make the world laugh. His reputation grew to the point where a doctor once gave a patient who complained of depression this simple prescription: "You must go to the music hall to see Joseph Grimaldi." The patient frowned and said: "I'm sorry, Doctor. It won't work. I happen to be Joseph Grimaldi."

We may laugh at the story but the fact is that depression is no laughing matter. Even clowns, even those whose business it is to make us laugh, they can and do suffer from depression. Depression happens to be a growing malady in these days and times in which we live. It's seen a startling increase over the past 40 years. It's 10 times as prevalent now as it was in 1960 and it strikes at a much younger age. That being said, that being the case, the question looms: "What are we to do? What are we to make of it?"

First of all we need to realize a distinction between normal depression and clinical depression. The latter needs to be treated by a professional and there are medications that are extremely effective. As far as normal depression is concerned, rare is the life that hasn't experienced it and rare is the person who hasn't had it touch their life.

I'm reminded of that Peanuts cartoon where the first panel has Lucy saying: "Sometimes I get depressed!" The next frame has Charlie Brown responding: "Lucy, life does have its ups and downs you know." The panels that follow have Lucy in a tirade. "Why does it have to be so? I want all ups, why can't I go from one up to another up. I just want ups, ups, and more ups." The strip concludes with a picture of Charlie Brown with a frown on his face and his hands on his hips and he's uttering his patented line: "I can't stand it!"

I believe our sentiments are with Lucy. We love to experience life with all ups, all roses and only good times. But I think Charlie Brown's view of life is much closer to reality. Depression is as much a part of it as happiness, failure as much a part of it as success, bad times as much a part of it as good times, the downs are as much a part of life as the ups.

When it comes to depression and the question of what are we to do and what are we to make of it, I think the very first thing is to recognize it as part of life, as something inherent to the human condition. Secondly, we need to give it respect; we need to give it time.

One of the calls I often get as a chaplain is to see a patient whom the nurse has determined to be depressed. Before I visit that patient, I always ask the nurse if there might be a reason for their depression. And I'm often told that the patient had just received bad news, that the patient was just informed as to the gravity of their condition. They expect that I'll cheer them up, that I'll soften their pain, but it wouldn't be right for me to do that. You see, their depression needs to be respected, their depression is appropriate given what it is they happen to be facing. Just as people need time to recover from surgery, people need time to recover from depression, they need time to be depressed.

When I do a memorial service at the hospital, I'll often begin by telling those who have gathered as to how many people had expected them to be over their grief the evening they returned from the cemetery. And I can tell by the nodding heads that, in fact, that was their experience. It seems we grant permission for people to be sad and depressed for three and maybe four days max. We expect them to quickly return to their bubbly selves. But in truth, they need more time. They need to absorb the trauma generated by what they had been told or what they had just experienced. We need to respect people's depression in the sense that we need to allow them time to be depressed.

We also need to realize that depression is not permanent. Barbara Johnson has authored a number of self-help books. She lost a son in Vietnam and another son was killed by a drunk driver. Besides that, her husband sustained a brain injury in a horrid automobile accident. Despite all that happened, Barbara learned to live again and did so with vigor and vitality. When asked how that was possible, she credited the biblical phrase: "It came to pass." When asked how that phrase proved helpful, she said it was simple, the phrase says "it came to pass," it doesn't say "it came to stay."

When we're bogged down with depression, when life has been such that one can't help but be depressed, it's important to remember that this, too, shall pass. Bad times like bad things are not here to stay, they're here to pass. In time, things will and do get better.

So when it comes to what we are to do and what we are to make of depression, we need first of all to recognize it as part of life, we need to respect the fact of its existence, we need to realize it's not permanent, and we also need to learn from its experience.

I read of two children who visited the cave section of Kentucky some time ago. As they were coming up from deep within the earth, they reached a certain spot from which they could look through an opening overhead into the darkness of the sky above. One of the children exclaimed: "Daddy, look! Even in this dark cave, I can see the stars shining."

It is an interesting fact that you can see farther in darkness than you can ever see in light. When the sky is bright and sunny, you might catch a cloud or two but your vision is limited to things around you. At night, however, you're able to see the stars and the moon and other galaxies. You can see a million miles into the universe.

From the vantage point of the darkness of depression, much is seen not visible before. There's much learned that was never learned before. Humility, compassion, understanding, fortitude are just a few of the virtues generated thanks to living in the darkness of depression.

I am reminded of that Robert Browning poem: "I walked a mile with pleasure; she chattered all the way but left me none the wiser for all she had to say. I walked a mile with sorrow and ne'er word said she but Oh! the things I learned from her when sorrow walked with me." Depression can be revelatory of thoughts and insights which good times could never provide.

And besides what depression can enable us to see, there's also the blessings which depression has been known to provide. John Wolf Schenk in his book *Lincoln's Melancholy*[2] offers a portrait of Abraham Lincoln as a man weighed down with depression not only during the years of the Civil War but throughout his life. The way Shenk's saw it, the depression forged a strength of soul that fueled his greatness. It spurred him to examine the core of his soul which in turn enabled him to look troubling reality straight in the eye. Lincoln became a great man and a great president thanks in no small measure to the depression from which he suffered.

In September of 1787, when Beethoven was but 16 years old, he revealed a malady that hounded him for the rest of his days. In a letter written soon after the death of his mother, he confessed that he suffered from depression. Many believe this depression acted as an inspiration for the symphonies he composed.

In late December of 1981 in a house out of Colts Neck, New Jersey; a man entered a room containing a chair, an old guitar, a harmonica in a holder and a simple four track tape recorder. He picked up his guitar and placed the harmonica holder on his neck. After a pause, he sang of loneliness and despair and hopelessness and he did so from the depths of depression. The name of the song was *Nebraska* and it became the title track of an album that would sell millions. Bruce Springsteen's album *Nebraska* stands as a grim testament to the power of melancholy for plumbing the bewildering depths of the human heart. Out of depression emerged a work of brilliance.

And how about that depressed songwriter who faced bankruptcy and poverty and ill health. Living in a rundown shack in a poor part of London, he's invited to compose a work for a charity benefit performance. Out of the depths of his despair and depression came that work we've come to know and love. The songwriter was Handel, the work was *The Messiah*.

Depression, through the years, has produced great people who in turn did great things and are responsible for unbelievable works of art and beauty. There is much gold to be plumbed from the depths of depression.

And then there are the antidotes for depression, the correctives for the melancholy, for the sadness that can pain a life. Karl Menninger, the famed psychiatrist, would take clients suffering from depression on five-mile hikes. He found that the walk brought more oxygen to the lungs, a bit of rose to the cheeks, and it circulated the blood. And besides that, it put the client in touch with nature and it was surprising how helpful that was in the lifting of their spirits.

When Viscount Grey, Britain's foreign minister during the First World War, was feeling down, he would leave London and go out into the country and there, in bird watching and listening to running brooks and the rustling of leaves, he was able to reinvigorate his drooping spirit.

And if the exercise of the body doesn't do it, there's always the exercising of one's soul. A Dr. Lynn Sherman studied nearly 200 patients after they lost a child. Her results showed significantly less depression amongst those patients who reinvested their energies in some selfless activity. Some volunteered to help others who lost a child. Some volunteered in some community organization that needed help. It was found that their ability to contribute to someone else's well-being helped reduce feelings of powerlessness and helplessness, two feeders of depression.

Dr. Bernie Siegel reported that senior citizens who volunteer their time and talents find that serving others gets their mind off their own aches and pains, two other feeders of depression. Dr. Alfred Adler said he could cure depression in fourteen days by, each day, sending the patient across the railroad tracks to a town nearby and there have them find someone in need and have them do all in their power to address that need.

Be it volunteering, be it just doing things for the sake of others, it's a way of exercising the soul and, like exercising the body, it's been shown to be a corrective for melancholy, a relief for depression, an antidote for despair.

And, finally, there's the matter of changing one's focus. I liked that story of the young husband in pursuit of a midnight snack. He enters the kitchen and turns on the light only to have the light bulb go dark. Bound and determined to pursue his goal, he decides to change the light bulb. He walks gingerly along the wall of the darkened kitchen to a closet to fetch the ladder and the bulb but, in the process, he overturns a dish of dog food and must painfully walk amidst the "kibble and bits" it contained. He maneuvers the ladder to the center of the kitchen and with light bulb in hand he ascends the ladder. It might have been a "kibble" or it might have been a "bit" had gotten lodged near the ball of his foot and when he stepped on the second rung of the ladder; he let out a howl and then crashed to the floor. At this point, his wife comes running down the stairs and enters the kitchen and turns on the light above the sink, a light he had entirely forgotten was there. And the moral of the story is: Before you concentrate on what's broken, take a look around and see as to what still works.

One of the biggest feeders of depression is precisely that problem. One gets to concentrating on all that is broken in life: the broken relationship, the broken job, the broken dream, the broken body. And if that is all that one is looking at, if that is all that's being focused upon, depression is inevitable. What's needed is a focus on what works, what's needed is to look as to what happens to not be broken, what's needed is to switch on the light we might have entirely forgotten was there.

I've been talking with you about depression because our first reading sets its tone. A better epitaph for depression cannot be found. "I've been assigned months of misery. I'm filled with restlessness. Troubled nights have been allotted me. I shall not see happiness again."

The saving feature for Job with all of his depression sits in a line he uttered several verses past the ones we heard today. The line: "I know that my Redeemer lives!" If we know our Redeemer lives, if we know Jesus is with us, we are connected to a God who is our rock and our stronghold, our buttress against the attempts of despair and depression to overwhelm us.

My friends, if you're in the midst of depression, if your depression, your loss, your illness has plunged you into melancholy; remember:

it's part of the ups and downs of life. Remember: it needs time to be absorbed. Remember: it's come to pass and not come to stay. Look for the stars its darkness might reveal. Exercise your body and mind and soul. Focus not on what's broken but on what still works. Remember our Redeemer lives and as such we need not fear, we need not despair, for God is with us.

And remember, as Holocaust survivor Carrie Ten Boom said, "There is no pit so deep that God is not deeper still."

Marveling

John 3: 14-21
"...Yes, God so loved the world..."

An ancient practice in need of restoration

I recently read that many years ago our ancestors used to go out walking, usually on a Sunday afternoon, sometimes alone, sometimes with a spouse, sometimes with the whole family and they called it going marveling. They would look for unusual rocks, unusual wildflowers or seashells or even four leaf clovers, whatever could be labeled as marvelous things. They would collect them and bring them home and then they'd show off the marvelous things to all whom they were close to or near.

As far as I know, no one goes marveling anymore. No one goes out on a Sunday in search of marvelous things. And that's a shame, because there's much to marvel about.

Take for example the foundations of the planet we call earth. Did you know that the earth rotates at a thousand miles an hour and if it rotated any slower or faster, we would all go up in flames? It's also a fact that the earth is tilted at a twenty three degree angle and, if it were off by one degree, we wouldn't experience the four seasons. If the crest of the earth were ten feet thicker, there would be no oxygen. If the moon was not where it happens to be, if it were a mile closer or further from where it presently is, we would be inundated by the tides or we'd have no tides at all either of which would spell a disaster for all concerned. If the earth had no ozone layer, we would all perish from the radiation of the sun. And if you buy the big bang theory as far as the creation of the solar system is concerned, scientists will tell you that if the fireball that exploded had exploded 1,000,000th of a second faster or slower, the earth and the other planets would not have evolved in the way that they did.

When it comes to marveling, we need merely to look at the facts I've just presented: the precise details of the earth's construction; the tiny margin of error that keeps destruction and disaster at bay, why it's a marvel to behold!

And consider as well the world of nature. Some years back, I watched one of those IMAX films and it featured the volcanic eruption of Mt. St. Helens. It was indeed a spectacular film as it seemed to take you into the heart of the volcano. One of the sobering aspects of the film was the panning of the area around the mountain following the eruption. It looked like a sea of volcanic ash. All you saw was mile upon mile upon mile of utter destruction. There was no sign of life anywhere. All of nature had been incinerated by the lava and ash of the volcano. What proved to be very interesting and awesome was the panning of that very same area today. You would not believe how green and robust and alive with wildlife that area has now become. Nature had, in essence, restored itself. What a marvelous thing to behold!

At the Cape Cod National Seashore, there are some interesting nature walks to partake in and each has a tale to tell as far as ecology is concerned. One of them leads down into a white cedar swampland. The cedar is extremely resistant to water rot and so when a swampy stretch is able to support any trees at all, the white cedar is the very first to grow there. Each year it sheds some of its foliage and this settles on the swampland and its residue gradually begins to build a base. As the swamp becomes firmer, maple trees begin to grow and shed their heavy foliage at an even faster rate until at last the swampland is no longer a swamp and other varieties of trees are able to move in. It's nature at work once again, not in restoration but in creation, and what a marvel that is to behold!

And did you know that when the huge tsunami hit the coastlines of the Indian Ocean on the day after Christmas in 2004, did you know that almost no bodies of animals were found amongst those of the thousands of people killed by that great wall of water? In Khai Lak, Thailand, elephants started trumpeting hours before the tsunami and, just before it struck, they fled to higher ground, some breaking free of the chains that held them. Similar animal behavior was reported in India, Sri Lanka, and Indonesia. Alert to the vibrating ground, alert to the sound and the scent of the ocean, members of the animal kingdom sensed imminent danger and made it to safety before any devastation took place. How marvelous a thing is that!

And how about the vase that was found near a mummy in an Egyptian tomb? When the vase was sent to a British museum, a worker noticed that in the bottom of the vase were a few hard shriveled peas. They had probably been in the vase for over 3000 years. The worker planted those peas and, in about a month, green shoots appeared. The 3000 year old peas had sprouted into new life.

And then how about the table made of apple wood which stood in a farmer's kitchen in New England for 60 years. One day a gnawing sound began to emanate from the table. It kept up for several weeks until at last a bug emerged from the table, unfurled its wings and took flight. An insect egg had been deposited in the trunk of the apple tree before it was made into a table and it remained in that wood all those years. Warmed, perhaps, by the heat of a coffee urn placed upon the table; it hatched and the little bug gnawed its way out.

If you want to go marveling, all you need do is look at nature, all you need do is look at the animal and the plant kingdom and you'd find so many things that are amazing, so many things that are mind boggling, so many things that could only be described as marvelous, fantastic, unbelievable.

And besides the world of nature, besides the antics of the plant and animal kingdom, there's much marveling to be done as well when it comes to the human kingdom, when it comes to those special individuals amongst us whose actions can leave us breathless, who do things that can only be labeled marvelous.

Of all the stories told about Mother Teresa, there is one that stands out. A Western reporter who was skeptical of her goodness went to Calcutta to see for himself if she was as good as everyone made her out to be. Arriving at the Hospice Center where she worked, he was told that Mother Teresa was busy attending to a dying beggar in one of the wards. As he neared where the dying man lay, he was repulsed by the man's sore covered emaciated body as well as by the stench of his decaying flesh. Yet, there was Mother Teresa with a water basin and a washcloth tending to the man's wounds. The reporter said to Mother Teresa: "I wouldn't do that for all the money in the world!" And Mother Theresa replied: "Neither would I!"

There are many Mother Teresa's working the corners of life and they do so at little or no pay. There are many Mother Teresa's attending to the people the rest of the world would just as soon forget. There are many Mother Teresa's doing work you or I wouldn't do for all the tea in China. And they are all, indeed, a marvel to behold.

Several years ago in Plains Hollow, New York, money for the Santa Claus Anonymous Fund was being raised, funds used to help poor children in the schools and in the community who would not have any Christmas presents were it not for that fund. There was a young boy in Plains Hollow Elementary School who had saved his pennies to give to the fund. On the Friday before Christmas, the last day to contribute to the fund, a heavy blizzard hit and the schools were closed. That young boy proceeded to walk for miles through the heavy snows to give the principal the 15¢ he had saved. As the principal accepted the small donation of the student, he could barely control his emotions for the young boy was on the list to receive presents from the fund.

You find so often unbelievable shows of generosity from those who can least afford to be generous. You'll find so often people with nothing giving up the little they have because there might be someone who needs it more than they. The little boy in that story and those like him are a marvel to behold.

And then there's that moving story of the man in his eighties who came to a doctor's office to have some stitches removed from his thumb. He told the nurse he was in a big hurry because he had an important appointment at 9:00AM that morning and he must not be late. The nurse took his vital signs and had him take a seat knowing it would be over an hour before anyone would be able to see him. The nurse noticed that the man kept looking at his watch urgently and she decided to see if she could help expedite his stay. She looked at his injured thumb and it looked good. It was healing nicely. She reported this to the doctor and he told her to remove the stitches and redress his thumb. As she was doing this, she and the older man got into a nice conversation. "So you have an urgent appointment at nine this morning?" She said. "Yes," he said, "The same appointment I have every morning. Every morning at 9AM I go to the nursing home to have breakfast with my wife." The nurse smiled and said: "You are such a handsome gentleman. I bet that's the highlight of her day." The man blinked and said: "She doesn't know who I am. She's had Alzheimer's disease for quite awhile now. She hasn't recognized me in the last five years." The nurse was surprised and said: "And you still go every morning even though she does not know who you are?" The man smiled, padded the nurse's hand and said: "She doesn't know who I am, but I know who she is." That kind of love is a marvel to behold.

Be it those Mother Teresa types. Be it those who can barely survive yet still give to the poor. Be it spouses whose love of their mate is nothing short of unbelievable. They are but a small sample of those who are amazing, those that do what is mind boggling, those who do things that can only be described as marvelous, fantastic, unbelievable.

If we were to take up that ancient practice of marveling, there would be plenty of things to marvel at. There would be plenty in the plant and animal and human kingdom that are a marvel to behold.

I've been cataloging a whole list of things we can marvel at because our Gospel contains one of the most marvelous lines you'll find anywhere in the Bible. It's the line that reads: "God so loved the world that he gave his only begotten son that whoever believes in him may not perish but may have everlasting life." God doing that for an ungrateful lot like ourselves is, indeed, a marvel to behold.

And what a marvel it is that all the things I've been talking about today have God's fingerprints all over them. Be it the recovery of Mt. St. Helens. Be it the germination of a three thousand year old seed or a sixty year old insect egg. Be it the exact distance of the moon from the earth. Be it a husband's dedicated love of an Alzheimer's stricken wife. Be it someone cleaning someone's flesh decayed body. Be it the generosity of one of the poorest kids in school. God's behind it all. God inspired it all. God's the reason it goes on. How marvelous is that?

What You Heard Said

Matthew 5: 17-37

"...You have heard that it was said..."

We need to be wary of what we hear.

I have no respect for justice. I maim without killing. I am cunning and malicious and gather strength with age. The more I am quoted, the more I'm believed. I flourish at every level of society. My victims are helpless; they cannot protect themselves against me, for I have no face and no name. To track me down is impossible. The harder you try, the more elusive I become. I am nobody's friend. Once I tarnish a reputation, it is never quite the same. I topple governments and wreck marriages. I ruin careers and cause sleepless nights. I make innocent people cry into their pillows. I make headlines and heart aches. In case you're wondering who I am, I am called gossip.

It's not so much gossip that I'd like to talk with you about today as it is what we hear. Our ears take in tremendous amounts of data. Rumors, alleged facts, whispered allegations and supposed truths are constantly begging entrance into those auditory canals we call our ears. We are constantly hearing what other people have to say and our hearing receptacles are privy to all sorts of information. And what is proven to be true more times than not is that what our ears are taking in is of a questionable nature. More times than not what our ears are processing happens to be in dire need of scrutiny.

So with that in mind, I'd like to suggest a few things to consider lest we be guilty of not screening the sorts of things gossip tends to deliver. James Randi, the famed magician, talked of going on a radio program to perform a minor experiment. Under an assumed name, he described how earlier that evening he had been driving through an area of New Jersey and had seen a V-shaped formation of triangular orange objects going overhead in a northerly direction. He wasn't sure if they emitted any noise because of the loudness of the traffic sounds around him. It was all, of course, a fabrication but within minutes, the switchboard of the radio station lit up like a Christmas tree. People were calling and claiming to have witnessed a similar sighting. Within a half an hour, the exact number of flying saucers had been established as well as their speed and altitude and the precise path of their direction.

What Randi did with the experiment was to show how a make-believe story can quickly get legs, how people will lay claim to something they could not have possibly seen because to begin with there had not in fact been a sighting of any unidentified flying objects.

One of the things to keep in mind when data and information pass through our ears is that maybe what's been taken in has no basis whatsoever in fact or reality. Maybe what's been heard was a fantasy which, as was the case with those callers at that radio station, a fantasy which had taken on a life of its own.

Another thing to keep in mind when data and information pass through our ears is that its source always needs to be taken with a grain of salt. When Jay Leno replaced Johnny Carson on the Tonight Show, he started to take some heat. Critics unfavorably compared him to Johnny and most thought that with all that criticism his stay as host would be short-lived. To bolster his spirits, Leno kept a stack of unpleasant reviews on his desk for inspiration. One review stated: "he asks too many soft questions." Another said: "he's being too nice." There were plenty of others not quite as kind. Those unpleasant reviews that Leno kept on his desk were actually written in 1962 and were directed at Jack Paar's replacement, an awkward nobody named Johnny Carson.

Producer Irving Thalberg strongly advised Louis B Mayer against buying the rights to the novel *Gone with the Wind*[3] because no Civil War picture had ever made a dime. Greg Lemont some years back won handily the Tour de France and that was after a critical headline that read: "he's fat and he's finished." And who can ever forget the talent scout who told Hollywood studios that Fred Astaire could dance a little but had no redeeming qualities. And then there was the teacher who told Thomas Edison's mother that he wouldn't amount to anything. Negative voices and negative comments often come through our auditory canals and, as evidenced by some I've just mentioned, their source needs to be taken with a grain of salt.

And what's true when it comes to the negative is true as well when it comes to the positive. I need but cite Hans Christian Anderson's tale of *The Emperor with No Clothes* [4] where two weavers promise the Emperor a fine suit of clothes that they will weave from an exquisite thread visible to all except those hopelessly stupid. When the Emperor receives that fine suit of clothes, he can't see it. But not wishing to be tagged hopelessly stupid, he pretends that he can. His subjects, his inner circle are afraid to tell the Emperor the truth, afraid to do anything but complement the Emperor on his clothes and that's precisely what they do. It's only when a young child blurts out the fact that the Emperor has no clothes that the truth dawns upon the Emperor and great embarrassment envelops his life.

Now it might well be that people treat us as the Emperor's subjects and inner circle had treated him. What we're told is not what we should be hearing but what we want to hear. So when it comes to the bits of data and information that comes through our ears, the source needs to be taken with a grain of salt for it may well be that he or she are not to be trusted when it comes to the accuracy of what it is they happen to be telling us.

Another thing to keep in mind when data and information come through our ears is its context. Some weeks back I quoted one of my favorite authors who described the news on television or on the radio or in print as a proctological view of life and by that he meant that most of the news reported as the events of the day represents the sewage portion of what went on that day.

Newspaper editors are constantly asked the question: "Why can't you print good news instead of the disasters and violence and crime that get all the ink?" And the answer, of course, is that they would not sell any newspapers if they did.

So if the context of the information and data coming through our ears is that of the television or radio or the evening news, what our ear happens to be receiving is by nature highly negative and not really representative of how most people actually behave and how most things actually are.

I catch on occasion the Jon Stewart show on Comedy Central and one night he played a clip which one of the talking heads on cable television happened to show on his evening program. The clip was of a prominent public figure saying something outrageous and it was hailed as exhibit A of the man's lunacy as well as his radical nature. What Stewart then did was to reverse the clip to its previous three minutes which wasn't aired on that cable program. Put the two together and what sounded silly and outrageous and radical didn't sound silly or outrageous or radical at all.

Who can forget the sudden firing of Shirley Sherrrod, an African American USDA official, when a news clip surfaced displaying her bias towards a farmer who happened to be white? Those who did the firing soon had egg on their face because it was learned later that day that the clip was the "sin" part of a sin and redemption story she had been relaying to a women's group whom she happened to be addressing.

Television and radio and the newspaper not only gives a proctological view of life but they also give us a slanted, prejudicial view of life and so the data and information coming through our ears may be tainted by a particular ideology not representative of the entire truth.

I read a respected journalist decry as to how too many of us listen to only one point of view which only serves to affirm our prejudice when in fact that prejudice needs to be challenged. So it's imperative when data and information come through our ears that we consider its context lest we be duped into believing what is not totally true and what happens to be lacking vital pieces of information.

Another thing to keep in mind when data and information comes through our ears is enlightenment. Popular thinking said the Earth was the center of the universe yet Copernicus studied the stars and the planets and proved mathematically that the Earth and the other planets in the solar system revolve around the sun. Popular thinking said surgery didn't require a clean set of instruments yet

Joseph Lister studied the high death rates in hospitals and introduced antiseptic practices which began to save lives. When I visited hospitals back in the 70s, popular thinking had patients who suffered a myocardial infraction being treated as a child. They were to restrain from any sort of activity even being told to refrain from lifting their arms. Hip replacement surgery required days of bed rest before any steps could be taken or any therapy could be started. And I recall, when I was young, a doctor telling an obese friend of mine to take up smoking to lose weight.

So much of the popular thinking of yesterday was fraught with error and outright ignorance and misunderstanding and so may well be the case when it comes to the popular thinking of today. We continue to learn. We continue to stumble upon truths previously unknown. We continue to be surprised by insights and discoveries which proved to be contrary to what had previously been believed. We need to account for enlightenment when it comes to the data and information passing through our ears for it may well be that what we heard may no longer be true.

And finally, there's the matter of authenticity. A very close priest friend of mine once received a call from the chancery regarding someone who contacted them claiming that he, my friend, had molested him. My friend was devastated for he never did such a thing Luckily, before the papers got a hold of it, the source was identified as an extortionist looking to reap financial gain from false and heinous accusations.

Who can ever forget Cardinal Bernadine's ordeal, the Cardinal being one of the most loved and finest of Cardinals of the 20th century. He made headlines in Chicago as he, too, had gotten accused of molesting a child. It would be two weeks and much angst and publicity later that the Cardinal was exonerated; the accusation would, however, go on to haunt him till the day he died.

A lot of data and information that enters our ears is not authentic, it's not based on truth and it would do us well to note that fact lest we think ill of someone undeserving of a malicious lie which we had been fooled into believing had contained a grain of truth.

In our Gospel today, Jesus unveils a whole new philosophy with each point beginning with the statement: "you heard it said." In essence, he was telling his disciples that there was more to what it was they heard, and he did so with the follow-up statement: "I say to you."

I believe that same teaching technique can be applied to us. Jesus could well be saying to you and I that what we heard said was a fabrication and I say to you, make sure you didn't help give a fantasy a life of its own. Jesus could well be saying that what we heard said came from unreliable and non-trustworthy sources. I say to you: take with a grain of salt the negative and positive feedback you happen to receive. Jesus could well be saying that what we heard said needs to be taken in context; I say to you: that there is another side to what you heard, another point of view you need to listen to, there's parts of a truth that got left out. Jesus could well be saying that what we heard said needs to account for enlightenment. I say unto you that you not be too quick to accept popular thinking. Jesus could well be saying that what we heard said was inauthentic with no basis in truth; I say unto you: don't pay heed to malicious lies.

My friends, pay heed to the description of gossip with which I began the sermon. Make it a point to always be wary of what you heard said.

Saying No!

Matthew 4: 1-11

"...You shall not put the Lord your God to the test..."

Saying 'No!' is not an easy task.

Back in the 1980s, some of you might remember an advertising campaign that encouraged young people to abstain from the use of drugs. It came with a popular slogan and directions to implement the slogan. "If someone wants you to take any illicit drug," so the directions went, "draw your breath just slightly; press your tongue to the roof of your mouth; begin to speak dropping your tongue and rounding your lips as you do. What should emerge is the word No!" "Just say No!" was the slogan: "Just say No!" became the name of the campaign. Nancy Reagan embraced it and promoted it when her husband was the president.

Now, it would be nice if saying No! was easy. It would be nice if drawing your breath and dropping your tongue and rounding your lips were a simple thing to do. But you know and I know that's not the case. You know and I know that saying No! requires an unbelievable and an extraordinary amount of courage. But when that courage gets mustered, when our rounded lips emit the word No!, many good things tend to happen and many bad things tend to be kept at bay.

First of all, saying No! can be a firewall for many a stealth virus that can infiltrate the computer we call life. In C.S. Lewis' Screwtape Letters[5], you read of senior devil Screwtape attempting to teach younger devil Wormwood the tricks of the trade. In one of his counsels, he tells Wormwood that if he wants to win someone over to hell, he merely has to get them to say Yes! to something small. "The road to hell is a gradual one," so said Screwtape. And of course, he is right. Experiment after experiment has shown that succumbing to little evils is the best precursor to falling prey to much larger ones.

I remember reading of Susanna Wesley, one of the great mothers in history. One day, one of her daughters wished to do something which was not altogether bad but which was not right. When the daughter was told not to do it, she appeared to not take it very well.

It just so happened that Susanna and her daughter were standing beside a dead fire. "I want you to pick up a piece of coal." said the mother. "The fire is out so it's not going to hurt you." "I know it's not going to hurt me," said the daughter, "but I don't want to pick it up because it's going to blacken my hand." "Precisely," said the mom, "that's precisely why you should not do what you wish to do. It may not seem bad. You won't get burned for doing it. But it will blacken your hand."

So many times when we should say No!, we don't. because we say to ourselves: "What's the harm of it?" "How is the little lie going to hurt me?" "How is the taking of that candy bar going to matter?" "How can a minor indiscretion be so bad?" And there's an ounce of truth in that, but that ounce of truth can blacken our hands, that ounce of truth may well be the little evil Wormwood was looking for to lead us down the path to hell, that ounce of truth can act like a stealth virus infiltrating and then destroying the contents of the computer we call our life.

Second reason why we should say no is that it can buy us valuable time. The late Harry Chapin made popular a song many years back. It was entitled <u>Cats in a Cradle</u>. In that song, Chapin sings of a father who has planes to catch and bills to pay and never seems to be able to find the time to do things with his son. The song's refrain has him telling his son how "he's going to get together with him real soon, we're going to have a good time then!" The song ends with a twist of fate. The busy man is now old and wants nothing more than to get together with his son, but the son turns out to be just like he was. The son tells him: "We're going to get together real soon, we're going to have a good time then!"

One of the perks of saying No! is that it buys time, it can free up time that could be spent with our families or could be spent with the people we love. Sometimes No! must be said to good things.

Sometimes No! must be said to promotions or work-related or extracurricular activities, all noble and grand and important. But the problem is that the busyness they foster, the time they consume, may well find us in the shoes of that father Harry Chapin immortalized in that song.

The third reason why we should say No! is that it may well be the most positive thing we can ever do. Dr. Frances Kelsey realized as much in her role as a new drug evaluator for the Food and Drug Administration. The year was 1960 and her first assignment was to assess a drug which could help induce sleep and also relieve morning sickness for mothers who were pregnant. Because it was widely used in Europe and the rest of the world, it was expected that Dr. Kelsey would automatically approve it and she was being pressured by some of the most powerful drug companies to do that very thing. Kelsey, however, knew there were serious flaws in the data concerning the drug's toxicity. She also had questions about the quality control of the manufacturer of the drug. Dr. Kelsey withheld approval. She said No! to some very powerful interest groups and it nearly cost her her job.

Later that year, reports began to surface from other countries across the world of babies being born with serious deformities from mothers who had used the drug. Thanks to Dr. Kelsey's No!, the drug Thalidomide never caused the devastation in America it caused across the world.

There are many circumstances where saying No! is the right thing to do but, of course, not the easy thing to do because more times than not it can antagonize an employer. It can sully our reputation. It can aggravate a friend. It can have us facing some serious pressure from very powerful sources. When saying No! is the right thing to do, it usually comes with a price, and the price can be very high.

The fourth reason why we should say No! is that it could well be the impetus for others to do the same. Some years ago, reporters were interviewing Boris Yeltsin asking what gave him the courage to say No! to communism, what gave him the courage to stand up to the leaders of the Kremlin. He pointed to Lech Walesa who not only said No! to communism but led an uprising of dockworkers to do the same. When they asked Lech Walesa what inspired him

Life Injections IV

to do what he did, he pointed to Martin Luther King Jr. and his saying No! to the segregation policies of the South. And when they asked Martin Luther King Jr. about the courage to say No!, he pointed to Rosa Parks who said No! to moving to the back of the bus.

Our saying No! could well have the same sort of inspirational power. Our saying No! may well be the spur necessary to get others to say No! Many an embedded sin, many an institutional evil, many a long-standing injustice have been allowed to continue because there were no Boris Yeltsin's, no Martin Luther King Jr.'s, no Rosa Parks' who were willing and courageous enough to say No!, willing and courageous enough to say in no way can this continue.

The fifth reason why we should say No! is that our health and well-being may lie in the balance. A story is told of a businessman who announced to his office one day that he was going on a diet. The very next day, however, he arrived at the office with a large coffee cake in hand. "What happened!" his colleagues asked. "We thought you were going on a diet." "I was," the man replied, "and I was on my way to the office this morning and I passed by a bakery and saw this incredibly sumptuous looking coffeecake on display in the window. So I prayed, God, if you really want me to have the coffee cake for breakfast this morning please find me a parking spot right in front of the bakery. And sure enough, there it was! The eighth time around the block, there it was!"

So many of the health problems we experience today are directly related to food. In some cases the kind of food, and other cases the quantity of food. The remedy rests in saying No! No to the extra helpings, no to the fried foods, no to the sugar laden donuts, no to the binges, no to the snacks and beverages loaded in calories, no to making that 8th trip around the block for the coffeecake we didn't need.

The obesity and cholesterol issues that plague our nation's health can find major relief with the persistence of No! at the refrigerators and the dinner tables and the banquet halls that frequent our day.

The sixth and final reason we should say No! is that it's often befitting of us as a Christian that we do. There's a marvelous story about the famous Berlin Wall at the time when bad blood existed between the adjoining cities. Those living on the eastern side decided one day to dump truck loads of stinking garbage over the wall. That not only infuriated the West Berliners but they demanded of Mayor Willie Brandt that he respond in kind, that he retaliate, that he exact revenge. Brandt said No!

What he did instead was request that everyone bring a flower to a specific place near the Berlin wall. Hundreds of beautiful flowers were thus gathered. He then had his people dump truckloads of those flowers over the wall while at the same time raising a banner which read: "We each give what we have."

Willie Brandt said No! to revenge, No! to responding in kind and offered instead a positive alternative. Saying no to revenge, saying no to despair, saying no to prejudice, saying no to bigotry, saying no to injustice, saying no to intolerance, that's just a sample of the saying of No! that it would be befitting of us as a Christian to do.

In today's Gospel, we hear the familiar story of the devil's temptations of Christ. To these appealing temptations, Jesus had the courage to say No! We pray at the beginning of the Lenten season for the same courage to say No! The courage to say No! to the harmless looking indiscretion that can blacken our hands and give the devil Wormwood the opening he needs. We pray for the courage to say No! to the demands on our time that take us away from our family, that can have us telling our child how "We're going to get together with them real soon, that we'll have a good time then!" We pray for the courage to say No! to that eighth trip around the block for that coffeecake we don't need. We pray for the courage to say No! to the varied injustices embedded in the systems around us thus inspiring others to do the same. We pray for the courage to say No! to revenge and despair and bigotry and all the stinking garbage that gets tossed over our walls. It is Lent! As a penance, learn to say No!

Quality of Friendships

John 15: 9-17

"...Instead, I call you friend..."

Friendships or lack thereof can make or break a life

I recently came across a list of the types of people we best not make a friend. Names were provided to describe their habits. On that list were the critics who constantly complain or give unwarranted advice; included as well were the martyrs who are forever the victim, forever whining in self pity. Also included were the wet blankets who are pessimistic and habitually negative not to mention the steamrollers who are blindly insensitive to others. Included as well were the gossips who spread rumors and leak secrets. And then there were the control freaks who are unable to let go and let things be, along with the backstabbers who are irrepressibly two faced. Also on the list were the green eyed monsters who seethe with envy as well as the volcanoes who build up steam and are primed for eruption. Last on the list were the sponges who are always in need but never give anything back and the competitors who always keep track of tit for tat. I believe it goes without saying as to why it would be best if we didn't make anyone on that list a friend.

I've shared with you that list because I'd like to talk with you today about friendship, talk with you about why friendships are important and why it is that we need to be careful as to whom we choose as friends. Friendships can make or break us. There's much in life riding on who it is we choose to be our friend.

Let's begin with the matter of our health. You may recall my telling you about one of the most interesting studies ever recorded. It was the study as to which city in America had the healthiest population. It proved to be Roseto, Pennsylvania. Their population had the lowest incidences of heart disease, the lowest incidences of the varied illnesses that plague the human race. Malcolm Gladwell in his best-selling book *Outliers* [6] referenced that study in his book's introduction.

Now, what made that study unique and interesting is that all that we associate with health: diet, exercise, environment, and genetics. None were the factor in the positive medical report the city received. The city was almost exclusively Italian. Pasta was consumed on a regular basis. Cigars with their billowing smoke could be found in the hands of a good number of the male population. And you'd be hard pressed to find a jogger, a vegetarian or anyone with habits conducive to good health. The one and only thing that separated Roseto, Pennsylvania from all the other cities included in the study were the close relationships which were part and parcel of the city, friendships in Roseto ran long and deep.

A research scientist at Duke University found that patients with heart disease and few friends were six times as likely to die within six months as those with heart disease and many friends. Another study unveiled the fact that people with a broad array of friendships are significantly less likely to catch colds than those with only a few whom they could call a friend. A large study in Alameda County California sought to determine the causes of poor health and, not unlike what was discovered in Roseto, Pennsylvania; they determined that it had little to do with their socioeconomic status or how often they saw a doctor. Their smoking and drinking and poor nutritional habits did not come into play. It all rested upon the number and degree of friendships. So one of the primary things riding on the quality of our friends is our health and well being. The more good friends we have, the healthier we will be.

Then there is the matter of wealth, not wealth in terms of dollars or cents, not wealth in terms of status or privilege or prestige, but wealth in terms of possessing what really matters when it comes to life.

I cite some comments made by author John Maxwell: You can build a beautiful house but eventually it will crumble. You can develop a fine career but one day it will be over. You may have a great sum of money, but you can't take it with you. You may be in superb health today, but in time it will decline. You can take pride in your accomplishments, but someone will surpass you. Discouraged? Don't be! For the one thing that really matters lasts forever and that one thing are the friendships we've accumulated in the course of our life.

Who can ever forget the lesson Clarence Oddbody taught George Bailey in that terrific movie *It's a Wonderful Life*. You might recall how George Bailey's troubles began when his absent minded uncle misplaced $8,000.00. Realizing he could go to jail for his Uncle's mistake and realizing the shame it would inflict upon his family; Bailey goes to the bridge at the end of town intending to jump to his death. As he put it, the world would be better off without him. It was then that his Guardian Angel Clarence Oddbody makes an appearance. To keep him from jumping, he shows Bailey that the world would not be better off without him and he does it by having him walk through Bedford Falls as it would have been had he never lived. As you might recall, it proved to be a pretty dismal place.

Buoyed now by the realization that his life did made a difference, he runs to his house and there in his house was the bank examiner looking for the missing money and so was the Sheriff who was there to arrest him should he fail to produce it. Bailey hugs and kisses his wife and children and before the examiner or sheriff can say anything, in walks Uncle Billy with a wicker basket filled with the money he collected from all of George's friends and he pours it on the dining room table. Right behind him come others, all of whom add money to the pile. There was Mr. Martini, owner of the local night club, who brought in the money from the club's jukebox. There was Mr. Gower, the druggist George worked for as a boy, who brought in all the money he made that day. Millionaire Sam Wainright sent a telegram promising cash to cover the missing money. With his house filled to capacity with all of his friends, in walks George's war hero brother who proposes a toast: "To my brother, the richest man in town!"

It was then that George Bailey eyed a copy of a book on top of the pile of money. He opened it and discovered it was a gift from

Clarence Oddbody, his Guardian Angel. The inscription read: "no man is a failure who has friends"

That final scene, that inscription, sums it up beautifully. Real wealth, true success, that which is of ultimate value doesn't come down to dollars and cents and it doesn't come down to what you've accomplished. And it doesn't come down to any of the things the world may claim to be of value. It all comes down to friendships. It all comes down to the quality of our friends.

I know of someone who keeps an Italian philosophy poem on his restaurant wall. It reads: "Count your garden by the flowers never by the leaves that fall. Count your days by golden hours, don't remember clouds at all. Count your nights by stars not shadows. Count your life with smiles not tears. And with joy on every birthday, count your age by friends not years."

And besides wealth and health, friendships may well insure our longevity. You may recall my telling you about an orchestra in Florida called the Senior Citizens Orchestra of Miami Beach. All of its members were over 60, a great many over 70, and more than a few were over 80. It was put together by a fellow named Henry Osman and he reported that the friendships which that orchestra created accounted for the fact that no one died in the first five years of the band's inception.

In a ten year study of people aged 70 and over, a network of good friends was found to increase longevity by an impressive 22%. Good friends can account for many a long life.

And good friends can also account for our hearing the truth, a truth that can set us free. I'm reminded here of a poster in a counseling office depicting a rag doll being squeezed through the rollers of one of those old washing machines. The caption read: "The truth shall set you free but first it will make you miserable." And of course, that's spot on. Truth has a way of making us miserable because it has us confronting what we'd just as soon not face and confronting what we'd just as soon not hear.

I'm reminded of something called an intervention. In essence, it's a group of friends who have gotten together because one of their friends has embarked on a self destructive path. Whether it be the abuse of drugs or alcohol, whether it be negative behavior or perhaps just arrogance, the friend in question needs to confront the truth and the group does its best to help him or her do just that, to help him or her to hear and face what had eluded their consciousness.

I believe it was a line from Camelot that went: "the uglier the truth, the truer the friend that will tell you." Many a man, many a woman, thanks to true friends are thriving today because those friends got them to accept and deal with the truth which in fact did set them free.

And the final reason why we need to insure the quality of our friends is the fact that our very life may well depend upon it. Professional basketball coach K.C. Jones was asked by Kevin McHale as to why he never congratulated or commended a player when they were turning in an outstanding performance. And his answer was that he didn't have to, that 15,000 fans and TV commentators and reporters were doing it for him. Then he went on to say that his job was to offer positive comments when nobody happens to be cheering.

It's when nobody is cheering, it's when life's bottom has been touched that friends prove quite valuable and more than a few have testified that without friends they never would have survived the unwanted and tragic news that fell upon their doorsteps. Kahil Gibran once remarked that we can forget those with whom we've laughed but we can never forget those with whom we have cried. True friends, quality friends, those with whom we've cried have helped more than a few of us get through what could have destroyed our life.

I've been talking with you about friendships because our Gospel today tells about the fact that despite our not deserving it, God has befriended us; God has labeled us his friends. By that fact, by that reality we are not only privileged and honored being that close to God's heart but we're also given a sense of the beauty and the value of friendship.

My friends: Choose your friends carefully. Avoid the wet blankets and the volcanoes and the steamrollers and the gossips. And then value and treasure those you've chosen. They will keep you healthy. They will make you wealthy. They'll enable you to live longer.

They'll keep you in touch with the truth. And one or more may in fact save your life.

The Morphing of Peace

John 14: 23-29

"...I do not give it to you as the world gives peace..."

Be wary of the kind of peace you may be looking for.

There once was a King who offered a prize to the artist who would paint the best picture of peace. Many artists participated and the King looked at all of the entries but there were only two pictures he really liked and he had to choose between them. One picture was of a calm lake with the lake acting as a mirror for the peaceful towering mountains that surrounded it. Overhead was a blue sky with fluffy white clouds. All who saw this picture thought it the one worthy of the prize. The other picture had mountains, too, but these were rugged and bare. Above was an angry sky from which rain fell and from which lightning flashed. Down the side of the mountain tumbled a foaming and raging waterfall. Nothing looked peaceful at all. But when the King looked closely, he saw behind the waterfall a tiny bush growing out of a crack in the rock. On the bush, a bird had built her nest. There in the midst of the rush of angry waters and the surrounding angry sky sat the bird upon her nest in perfect peace.

Now, if it were up to us to choose the best picture of peace, my guess is that the first picture is the one we'd choose. And who can argue with that choice, given the noisy and turbulent and hectic and loud world in which we happen to live. There's not a person amongst us who wouldn't like to escape to a calm lake with peaceful towering mountains surrounding it and with no cell phones or pagers or alarm clocks or televisions or screaming kids to spoil its serenity.

But as much as we might value and long for and cherish that particular kind of peace, it's not without its dark side. What passes for serenity is often not the nirvana it's considered to be.

Take the magnificent poem <u>The Rhyme of the Ancient Mariner</u> by Samuel Taylor Coleridge. In that poem, a mighty sailing vessel gets caught in a terrible storm. Petrified, the sailors pray for relief from the violence and the turmoil. Eventually, their prayer gets answered as their ship is blown into a perfectly calm sea. Everyone is ecstatic. Peace at last! But then gradually, the men come to realize that the calm and the peace proved to be no blessing at all. Their ship, in Coleridge's words, "is as idle as a painted ship upon a painted ocean." With no turbulence or wind to speak of, the ship will never leave the spot it is in. It'll be stuck there forever.

In much the same way, when peace comes over us, it may in fact mean we've secured a spot that we will never leave. That we've come to a point in our life where we choose to stay just the way we are leaving undeveloped and untapped a gift or a talent for which it would be a shame that no one will ever see it.

I heard of a famous motivational speaker who was conducting a seminar for a large number of participants. He asked for three of the participants to volunteer and then he invited them upon the stage. He asked them to introduce themselves to the audience and explain what kind of work they happened to do. The participants did just that and it happened that one was a lawyer, one was a nurse, and one was a mechanic. He then asked each of them the same question. "When you're lying in a coffin in a funeral home with your friends surrounding you, what do you hope they will say? The lawyer said: "I hope people will say that I was a fair and just lawyer. I hope my clients will say I was an honest and an upright man." The nurse replied: "I hope my patients will say that I was caring and warm and nurturing and compassionate. I hope they will say as to how I attended to their needs." The mechanic said: "If I was lying in a casket with my friends surrounding it, I hope I would hear someone say 'I think I see him breathing.'"

The kind of peace exhibited in the first picture, that peace which many of us cherish and desire and long for can morph into the peace of death. It can morph into a peace where a gift or a talent sits idle, where tremendous potential sits untapped. It can morph into a peace that has the earmarks of stagnation, where an individual looks as though they've died even though they happen to still be breathing.

The kind of peace exhibited in the first picture can also morph into appeasement. A few years ago a widely aired commercial showed Michael Jordan shooting a basketball by himself in a gym. In a voice over, narrated by Jordan, the viewer learns of all the thousands of shots he's missed and the hundreds of games he's lost. The commercial concludes with the punch line: "Dare to try!"

Unfortunately today there are many parents who do not dare to try and do anything that might upset their child. They do not dare to say no. They do not dare to let them experience failure. They do not dare to punish them. They do not dare to have them suffer the consequences of their actions. And all for the sake of peace and tranquility.

Soren Kierkegaard tells the story of a schoolboy who refuses to learn. His teacher tries hard to get him interested in his schoolwork and to apply himself to his studies but nothing came of it. The boy paid her little attention. Yet, she persisted. She begged him to cooperate. She pleaded with him to let her teach him but he refused. Eventually the teacher says: "Okay! Tell me what you want to do and you can do it." The boy says: "All I would like to do is sit in the back of the room, do some drawings, sleep a little bit and come and go as I please." And the teacher said: "Fine! You can do it." Kierkegaard ends the story by saying: "The boy got what he asked for because the teacher had given up on him."

Giving our children everything they want, never telling them No! shielding them from upset, is in essence giving up on them. It's denying them the fuss, the disappointment and the pain and the sacrifice that he or she needs to experience so that they will become something other than the spoiled brat into whom they'll eventually evolve.

Not daring to try and put any limits on a child's activity, all for the sake of peace and tranquility, is giving up on that child's chance to be bigger and better and greater than they will be if turmoil and upset are shielded from their life.

The third problem with the peace exhibited in the first picture, the peace which many of us cherish and desire and long for is that it can morph into a veil for a tiny and sad and lonely life.

It has been said that we have a choice in life, we can choose as to whether we want a broken heart or a shriveled heart. If we give of ourselves to anyone, a child, a spouse, a friend, or a community, than sooner or later our hearts are going to break. And the only way to keep our hearts from breaking is by being careful not to give our hearts to anyone, not a child, not a spouse, not a friend, a community or even a dog. If that's what we choose to do, then something worse than a broken heart will happen, our hearts will become dried up, desiccated, and empty of love.

Now when it comes to peace and tranquility, the shriveled heart is the way to go. It will mean we won't have to suffer the disturbance of an Alzheimer's stricken wife or the upset of a wayward teenager or the agony of an unfaithful spouse. It will mean we won't have to suffer the pain of burying a husband or the trial of having our sleep broken by a crying child or the upset of a day spent in worry because someone we love is sick. Minus all those heart rending and heartbreaking experiences, those who choose a shriveled heart live a fairly peaceful life but, Oh! what a tiny sad and lonely and empty life that happens to be.

The fourth problem with the peace of that first picture, the peace most of us cherish and desire and long for is that it can morph into apathy Tony Campolo is an evangelical preacher whom I've had the pleasure of hearing on several occasions and he ranks, in my opinion, amongst the top churchmen of this country. In a chapel service at a conservative church college, he began his remarks by saying: "According to United Nations' statistics 10,000 people starved to death last night and most of you don't give a crap." But instead of using the word crap, he used a more vulgar word that means the same thing and a loud gasp overtook the entire congregation. He then looked at them all and said: "The problem with all of you is that you are more upset about the word I just used then you are about the fact that 10,000 people starved to death last night.

Compolo's hard hitting words are unfortunately true when it comes to far too many of us. Far too many of us fail to get upset over world hunger. Far too many of us fail to get upset over the extent of world poverty. Far too many of us fail to get upset over homelessness or the genocide in Darfur. Our peace and tranquility in the midst of the grave injustices and problems that plague our world and our society is a scandal. It speaks of apathy and indifference which is a shameful state of mind for someone claiming to be a follower of Christ.

And besides its morphing into apathy and indifference, that peace we cherish and desire and long for, the peace of the first picture could also morph into denial and suppression. There is a little parable in which a man who is window shopping can't believe his eyes when he sees a sign bearing the name "Truth Shop". He immediately enters and a polite salesperson asks him as to what type of truth he wished to purchase. Did he want partial truth or the whole truth? "Why, the whole truth," the man replied. "It's going to cost you!" said the salesperson. "What's it going to cost me?" asked the man. And the salesperson replied: "it's going to cost you your security."

Peace and tranquility go hand in hand with security and as that parable duly noted, the truth about ourselves comes at the cost of our security and, that being the case, it comes at the cost of our peace and tranquility as well.

Quite often what passes for peace and tranquility is often a cover for a life that is a lie, a life that has denied a sin or a foible or an issue or an emotion whose suppression has probably taken its toll on that life as well as the lives of those close by or near.

Going back to the story with which I began, the King ultimately chose the bird in her nest as the best picture of peace because, as he put it, peace does not mean to be in a place where there is no noise or trouble or hard work. Peace means to be in the midst of all of those things while at the same time being calm at the center of one's heart.

That is precisely the peace Jesus was talking about giving his disciples in today's Gospel, a peace totally different from the one the world happens to give which could best be described as the peace reflected in the first picture with its calm lake mirroring the peaceful mountains around it.

So my friends, if its peace and tranquility you're looking for, seek the peace of Christ. It's a peace that won't morph into stagnation or appeasement, that won't morph into a veil for a shriveled heart, that won't morph into apathy or indifference or denial or suppression. It'll be a peace that will endure the discomfort of tapping a talent as yet unseen. A peace that dares to try and disturb a teenager. A peace that won't get shaken when the whole truth is purchased. A peace that will be upset about world hunger. A peace that can cope with a broken heart.

My friends, if it's peace you are looking for, choose the peace of the second picture and not the first.

Attention Deficit Disorder

John 1: 29-34

"...Behold the Lamb of God..."

The importance and the value of sustaining our attention.

There is an old joke about a farmer who bought a mule guaranteed to listen to whatever it was told to do. The farmer told the mule to pull his plow but the mule refused to budge. The farmer yelled at the beast, pleaded with him, cajoled him but to no avail. Frustrated, the man called the previous owner to come over. "I thought you said this mule listened to whatever you told him to do but, in fact, he won't listen to me at all." Not saying a word, the former owner walked away and returned with a big stick. He took the stick and swatted the mule once across his rear end and, immediately, the mule began to pull the plow. "See," said the man, "he listens real good but first you've got to get his attention."

It's attention I'd like to talk with you about today, more specifically paying attention that I'd like to speak with you about today. Attention Deficit Disorder (ADD) is not a malady that only strikes children, but it's a malady that seems to have stricken a good part of the adult population of this country. We're finding it more difficult to sustain our attention, more and more difficult to maintain our attention. And it's taken its toll in many different ways.

First of all, it diminishes us. William H Hinson tells us why animal trainers carry a stool when they go into a cage of a lion. They have their whips, of course, and their pistols at their sides but most importantly they also carry a stool. Hinson says it is the most important tool of the trainer. He holds the stool by the seat and thrusts its legs toward the face of the wild animal. Those in the know maintain that the animal tries to focus on all four legs at once. In the attempt to focus on all four, a kind of paralysis overwhelms the animal, he becomes tame, weak, and disabled; all the result of his attention being fragmented.

As much as we pride ourselves as multitaskers, the truth is that the more we fragment our attention the less efficient we become, the more prone we become to making mistakes. A neuroscientist at Vanderbilt University found in his research that the human brain has a core limitation and that limitation is the inability to concentrate on two things at the same time. And so, if we, like those caged lions, are trying to pay attention to four things at the same time, it will most definitely diminish us. So when we can't sustain our attention because of the multiple tasks we're called upon to do, it will take its toll on the product of our labor. It will hamper our efforts to perform to the best of our ability.

Another way it can take its toll is the shortchanging of our family and friends. There's a story that has been repeated often. It is of a young warrior who came to his tribe's medicine man and told him: "Inside my head two dogs are fighting all the time. One is wise and beautiful and the other is ugly and rabid. Which one will win?" The medicine man answered: "The wise and beautiful one will win." "How do you know that?" asked the warrior. "Because that is the one you'll feed!" was the reply.

Whatever gets fed our attention is bound to do well. Whoever it is that we pay attention to is likely to positively benefit by that attention. You might recall my telling you of an experiment that took place involving ten students at a particular school. The entire school and been given an IQ test before the end of the previous year and these were identified as the ten who recorded the highest score. Teachers were told who the ten were and it was hoped that they would make it a point to pay them the attention they needed to excel. Sure enough, at the end of the school year, all ten were at the top of their class. The irony was that those ten students did not have the highest IQ scores. There were chosen at random. It had all been an experiment. What accentuated the rise of those ten students boiled down to the attention they were given by their teachers.

Many a child, many a friend, many a family member may well have done a lot better in life, may well have excelled, had they been fed attention, had they been fed individual and undivided and unfragmented attention. When it comes to our inability to sustain our attention, one of the tolls it can take is the shortchanging of our family and friends, the impeding of their potential, holding them back from realizing the gifts and talents embedded inside them.

Then there is the toll our ADD can take on the worth and dignity of those who happen to be in our company. Ted Koppel no longer has the TV airtime he once commanded but he'll go down in television history as a consummate interviewer, perhaps television's best inquisitive reporter. And what made him that was the rapt attention which he paid to all whom he interviewed. That rapt attention allowed him to hear what might've otherwise been missed and many a Koppel guest felt honored to be given that kind of attention.

The Wall Street Journal reported that a school sent a letter to parents in preparation for teacher conferences. Among the instructions was a strongly worded statement which read that under no circumstances should a parent answer a cellular phone during the conference. The point, of course, being that their child's welfare is too important to be absent a parent's rapt attention. .

I remember reading of an entertainer who had fallen upon hard times. She was no longer the singer she once had been. One day while singing to a less than enthusiastic audience, she finished her set and was then taken aback when the noise of the audience came to an abrupt halt. The bass player of the band was doing a number and it caught their undivided attention. He's doing his thing, he's really into it and that fallen entertainer, the singer who had just finished her set, was resenting it. She was jealous that he was able to do with his instrument what she couldn't do with her voice. She walked to his side and he glances in her direction expecting a smile. Instead she yawns in his face; she delivers what could be called the ultimate put down.

Our not sustaining our attention when in somebody's company can be likened to that yawn from that fallen entertainer. We may not be deliberately providing the ultimate put down but very subtly that's what we're doing whether we realize it or not. When things like cell phone calls and text messages have us immediately jumping to their attention, it usually tells the person in our company that they're not worthy enough, not important enough to receive that same kind of attention.

And then when it comes to the toll our ADD can deliver, there are the important things, the hidden messages that it would have been good for us to know and realize had it not been for our inability to sustain our attention. The late Jesuit Anthony De Mello had a vignette in one of his books involving a man whose marriage was in trouble. He sought the help of the Zen master who advised him to learn to listen to his wife. The man took the advice to heart and returned after a month to say that he had learned to listen to every word his wife was saying. The Master said to him with a smile, "now go home and listen to every word she isn't saying."

The famed psychologist M. Scott Peck said he was trained early in his studies that what the patient does not say is more important than what he or she does say. I was taught in chaplaincy training to always be alert for the red herring that might come swimming by in a conversation with a patient. The red herring being the throwaway remark that telegraphs what was really bothering the person we were talking to.

What all this means is that the inability to sustain our attention will all too often lead to our missing what the other person may be subtly trying to tell us, our missing cries for help, our missing key marks of discontent, our missing how the other person really feels, all of which can later lead to deep regret.

Also when it comes to our ADD, when it comes to our inability to sustain attention, there is the toll it can take when it comes to opportunity. According to the legend, if you find this touchstone on the coast of the Black Sea and hold it in your hand, everything you touch will turn to gold. You can recognize that touchstone by its warmth. All the other stones feel cold but that touchstone when picked up would quickly turn warm in your hand.

Once a man sold everything he had and went to the Black Sea in search of that touchstone. He began picking up every stone he could find on the coastline, wanting desperately to find the one that would lead to the golden touch. After some days pass, he realized he was picking up the same stones again and again, so he devised a plan: pick up a stone and if it feels cold, throw it into the sea. This he did for weeks on end. One day he came early to continue his search. He picked up one stone, it was cold and he threw it into the sea. He picked up another, then another and then another. They were all cold and he threw them into the sea. He then picked up yet another stone. It turned warm in his hand but, before he realized it, he threw it into the sea. He had it in his hand and he threw it away. Routine had dulled his attention and, as a result, what he longed to have was lost forever.

So it can go with almost every opportunity. Unless we're paying attention, unless we give our search for opportunity our undivided attention, the opportunity we were hoping to find may well pass us by and, like that touchstone, it will be lost forever. Our ADD may well keep us from that chance to make our dream come true.

Then finally when it comes to the toll that's taken when we're unable to sustain our attention, there's the missing out on the presence of God.

In the film *Bruce Almighty*, Jim Carrey portrays Bruce, a down and out reporter who was given the power of God after meeting God in the guise of a janitor played by Morgan Freeman. When Bruce becomes overwhelmed by the responsibility of his divine power, he longs to become a simple human being once again. He meets up with God in an empty office building and God is gracious enough to grant his request. As the janitor God ascends a ladder and is about to disappear beyond the ceiling, Bruce desperately asks where he is to look if he needs his help in the future. God looks back and says: "Just don't make the mistake most people make, they keep looking up."

God is not in some place up above, God's all around us and God often makes his presence felt. But if we're not paying attention, unless we're sustaining our attention, God may well pass us by and we'd be none the wiser.

That's what happened to two of John's disciples in today's gospel. If it wasn't for John saying: "Behold!" which loosely translated means "Pay Attention!" Jesus would've walked right past them and they'd be none the wiser.

So my friends, take a break from your cell phone and text messaging and your multitasking and pay attention. The product of your labor may well see a marked improvement. You'll not shortchange your child's potential. You'll have affirmed the worth and dignity of the person you're talking to. You'll not have missed the red herring in that conversation nor miss the opportunity you are looking for. You'll not have missed God making his presence felt. My friends, it's time you took care of your attention deficit disorder. Pay attention, sustain your attention, and give your cell phones and your Ipods a needed rest.

Excellence

Matthew 22: 1-14

"...how is it you came here not properly dressed..."

Excellence should be our constant pursuit.

L'Oreal of France has been described as a total beauty care company that combines the latest in technology with the highest of quality for the ultimate in products designed to beautify its users. Juliana Margulies of *The Good Wife* has recently signed on as one of its spokespersons. L'Oreal happens to have a hair coloring product which, in their words, will result in hair rich in color with zero gray. The brand name for the product is Excellence.

Well, it's excellence I'd like to talk with you about today. Not excellence as a beauty care product line, but excellence as a goal, excellence as a pursuit, excellence as a way of life. I believe God calls each of us to work to the best of our ability, to never be satisfied with mediocrity, to strive for excellence always. And when we heed that call, we stand to accrue many a blessing.

First of all, whatever we do will be well received. There's a children's book entitled *Good Lemonade* [7] and it tells the story of a boy named Hank who sets up a lemonade stand in front of his house. During his first few days on the job, Hank attracts only a handful of customers and no one comes back for more. So he then employs several gimmicks designed to attract customers. He offers discounts; he paints the cups, and lures two girls to dress up as lemons. After a week of finagling, Hank makes but a few sales.

Then Hank discovers that another kid down the block set up a lemonade stand and there is a long line of customers every day. Hank decides to stand in the long line to find out why the other kid is selling so much more lemonade than he. When he finally tastes the lemonade, his eyes light up. It is really good lemonade. That prompts Hank to spend the entire day shopping for the best of lemons, the finest of sugars, the highest quality water. He then proceeds to spend hours making sure everything gets mixed properly and in proper proportions. It's not long before he finds a long line of kids in front of his own stand waiting for a cup of his now "excellent" lemonade.

Although that story hails from a children's book, its lesson holds true. Excellence sells. One of the reasons why many years back American automakers saw more people buying Japanese cars than their own was because they held onto the attitude: "If it's not broke, don't fix it." whereupon Japanese automakers held onto the attitude: If it's not perfect, keep working on it."

My dad built his grocery business around excellence. When I would go with him to the Clinton Bailey Market to buy produce, I would watch him painstakingly go from stand to stand looking for the finest of produce money could buy. My dad never believed in bargains because he felt that what he could afford to sell at a reduced price wasn't worth selling. My dad never made a fortune in the grocery business but he made enough to put both my brother and I through college. For 35 years, my dad ran a successful business because it was based on excellence.

The first benefit of giving our best and pursuing our best, the first blessing of excellence is that it will be well received. Success will follow. Another benefit, another blessing is that there will be no regrets.

National Football League legend George Halas once said that nobody who ever gave their best regretted it. I always liked that story of an elderly carpenter who was ready to retire. The carpenter told his employer his retirement plans, his leaving the house building business. The employer was sorry to see him go but begged him to stay on long enough to build just one more house as a personal favor to him. The carpenter very reluctantly agreed. Instead of maintaining his usual high standards on his last job, he cut corners. He did sloppy work. He used inferior material. It was an unfortunate way to end a dedicated career. The carpenter finished his work, and the employer came to inspect what he had done. Then, to the carpenter's shock, his employer handed him the keys. "This is your house," he said, "It's my retirement gift to you."

Those who do things halfheartedly, those who cut corners and fail to work to the best of their ability often find, as did the carpenter, that there can be consequences to such behavior. It's not unusual for them to be filled with regret that they hadn't done their best. George Halas was indeed correct when he said that nobody who has ever done their best regretted it.

And besides excellence assuring no regrets, it can also assure positive behavior. Every husband in America will tell you that his wife is happier, friendlier and more productive after she's come home from a trip to the beauty parlor or after donning a dazzling new set of clothes. A nursing home, thanks to a grant from the Dallas Geriatric Institute and Mary Kay cosmetics, began doing weekly facials and almost immediately began seeing a definite improvement in the self image and the attitude of the elderly ladies who were living there.

I remember Father John Alderson telling me that when Timon High School introduced a dress code for students some years back, he saw a marked improvement in student behavior on many fronts. The discipline problems went down considerably and teachers found students paying far greater attention to the lessons they taught, and the grade point average for each student saw a constant rise.

I'll never forget being part of a search committee for a new executive director for the Life Transition Center. It was a blue ribbon committee; I was the low man on the totem pole. We interviewed 10 candidates and there was one who had all the credentials we were looking for, more so than the others. As we discussed our hiring her, one woman on the committee, an elegant one I might add, brought up one negative. She said that her dress had a few wrinkles and her hair wasn't done right. None of us noticed that, and as much as it bothered her, she wouldn't stand in the way of our selecting that candidate for the job.

We hired her and one year later we fired her because she missed grant deadlines, she didn't follow through on several of the things we had asked her to do. The wrinkles on her dress, her unkempt hair proved to be a sign of her lack of interest in quality and that lack of interest became evident in her work.

It's been said that if it walks like a duck, it eventually becomes a duck; if it flies like an eagle, eventually it becomes an eagle. When there is high quality, be it in dress, or appearance or work, it will often translate into high quality in behavior. Excellence has a way of making for improved activities in all facets of life.

And besides excellence assuring no regrets and positive behavior, excellence also breeds excellence. I learned recently an interesting bit of history. When Beethoven wrote his music, there wasn't the equipment or the technology available that could do his music justice. When he wrote the Solo of the C Minor Concerto, it was played on what was described as a musical box of wires, hardly more sonorous than an old beat up piano. One could say that Beethoven wrote music that could not be adequately rendered with the instruments of his time.

What his beautiful music did was to spawn the creation of greater and grander techniques and instruments. As his biographer pointed out "born into a day of small things, he helped the day to expand by giving it creations far beyond the scope of its available means of expression." Beethoven's creations of beauty inspired the further creations of things beautiful. Many years later, Beethoven's music would bring about an orchestra that could play it and resounding heart lifting instruments that would bring its magnificence to light.

Consider if you will the Olympic records set by some of the most excellent of athletes the world has ever produced. Those records never hold for very long. That's because the athletes who set them inspire others to excel, to rise to greater heights, to eclipse the bar for excellence that had previously been set.

I read where Mark Spitz, who won seven gold medals for excellence in swimming, I read that his record setting time back in 1972 would not have been good enough to qualify him for the most recent Olympic Games.

I read where the 100 meter speed skating record set by Dan Jansen in 1994, I read where that record time would've placed him in 40th place in the most recent of winter Olympics.

I'm reminded of the observation someone made who visited an art gallery in which stood an old Greek statue of Apollo, a beautiful figure of physical excellence. That someone said that he didn't know what was more impressive to him, to look at the statue or to watch the crowd as they looked. Invariably, everyone who stood before it even for a casual instant began to straighten up, pull back their shoulders, and stand tall. Excellence time and again causes others to push up to greater heights themselves. Excellence breeds excellence.

And then, finally, excellence exposes truth. I recall here the powerful scene of the movie *The Pianist*. The main character, the pianist was played by Adrien Brody who won an Oscar for his performance. The scene I'm referring to finds the pianist starved, emaciated and broken wandering through the rubble of a bombed out village. He'd been running from the Nazis for weeks on end and he takes refuge in an old abandoned building that was still standing in the midst of the rubble.

Soon afterwards, a Nazi captain enters the building and discovers him there. The pianist expects the worst but the captain recognizes him and there's a piano standing in the shambles of that building. The captain asks him to play and the pianist plays Chopin and he fills the dusty destitute room with the magnificent tones of one of his symphonies. The Nazi captain is spellbound by the elegant music. A transformation overtakes him as the beauty of what he is hearing stands in direct contrast to the severe devastation all around him. The excellence of the music exposes the absurdity of war; the absurdity of the terrible things war has done. It makes the thought of killing or capturing the Jewish pianist utterly ridiculous. The captain gives the pianist his jacket and exits the building.

In C.S. Lewis's *Chronicles of Narnia*[8], specifically *The Silver Chair*, as people watch the King, the hero Aslan, meet the crown prince, Aslan appears so bright and real and strong that everything else begins to look pale and shadowy compared to him.

Excellence has a way of exposing darkness. It's the straight stick you put next to the crooked one to show how disfigured it happens to be. Excellence exposes the truth of how absurd, how repulsive, how disgusting, how shallow is so much of what lies beside it.

The King in our gospel today is pretty upset with the man not dressed in a wedding garment. In particular, he was upset that the man came to the wedding dressed in less than his best. It served as Jesus' way of calling his hearers to pursue excellence, of letting it be known how upset God becomes when what we do and how we act is less than the best of which we are capable.

I reference here Martin Luther King Jr. who once said that if an individual is called to be a street sweeper, he or she should sweep streets even as Michelangelo painted or Beethoven composed music or Shakespeare wrote poetry. He or she should sweep streets so well that all the hosts of heaven and earth will pause and say here lived a great street sweeper who did their job well.

My friends, heed God's call to excellence. You'll have no regrets. You'll advance excellence. What you do will be well received. You'll expose the ugliness around you.

L'Oreal has the brand Excellence. May excellence be our brand.

Imperfection

Mark 6: 7-13

"...shake the dust from your feet as you leave..."

Perfection may well be a prize not worth claiming.

A disciple asked the Zen Master as to why he never married. The Zen Master replied: "When I was young, I was in search of the perfect woman. And in Cairo, I met a woman. She was beautiful and intelligent but unkind. And in Baghdad, I met a woman. She was generous and gracious but we had nothing in common. This happened again and again until finally I met a woman who was perfect. We had everything in common. She was generous, gracious, beautiful, intelligent." "Then why did you not marry her?" asked the disciple. The Zen Master replied: "Well, it was sad; you see, she was looking for the perfect man."

It's the perfect I'd like to talk with you about today. Not the perfect man or the perfect woman, but perfect in general and perfection in particular. There are many fixated on perfection. There are many striving to be perfect. And as commendable and as laudable as that may be, the perfect can often pale in comparison to the imperfect. Perfection can often be a prize not worth claiming. .

Dr. Halford Lucock tells a delightful story about a man who complained that he could never get caught up. Every day for 20 years he looked at his desk piled high with unfinished business, piled high with letters that needed to be answered and bills that needed to be paid and files that needed to be processed. When he walked out of the house to get away from the clutter, there was the grass that needed to be cut, the hedges that needed to be trimmed. "If only I could get caught up," he prayed, "if only I could get caught up." One night, he goes to bed and has a dream. In that dream, he was in a large room with a beautiful mahogany desk, clean, bright and shiny. On it, there were no letters or scraps of paper, no bills, no problems, and no files that needed to be processed. Out the window he could see the lawn and the hedges neatly trimmed, everything meticulously manicured. It was a great relief. He had caught up at last. "Thank the Lord," he said, "I'm caught up at last, peace at last."

But then in the midst of this seeming paradise, there nibbled a little question: "What do I do now?" The postman came down the street whistling and he figured he'd have mail for him to read. He hailed him and found that the postman's bag was empty and he was just out for a walk. He asked post man: "What is this place?" "Why don't you know?" said the postman. "This is hell!"

That's a story out of the imagination of Dr. Halford Lucock but it does make you think. If we lived in a perfect world where all the problems are solved and all the mysteries are gone, if we lived in a perfect world where there were no deadlines to meet or no work to do and we're all caught up with everything, why we'd be bored out of our minds. We'd be looking for things to do. We would in fact be in the midst of a living hell.

The imperfections of life are often the stimulants for life. They are what get us out of bed every morning. They are what prompts us to get busy. They are the incentives for doing what gives meaning and purpose to our life.

And also when it comes to the imperfections of life, there's the fact of its bringing out the best within us. I don't believe there is any question as to Michelangelo's secure position in the history of art. He stands head and shoulders above the sculptors of all time. His many masterpieces stand in testimony to his greatness.

As great and as magnificent as were the sculptured creations of Michelangelo, he himself was never satisfied with his work. After completing *Moses*, claimed to be his greatest work, the master sculptor surveyed what he created and then suddenly in anger he struck the knee of the statue with his chisel. And that was because it was less-than-perfect.

Michelangelo never did realize perfection in his lifetime and we can thank God that he never did because imperfections may well have been what fueled his drive for excellence. Imperfections may well have been what drove him to create many a beautiful sculpture and many a wonderful work of art.

So not only have imperfections been the stimulant for life itself, but they've also been the stimulant for many a magnificent piece of art or magnificent bar of music or magnificent poem. Many an artist or musician or poet may never have reached the pinnacle of their profession had it not been for imperfections driving them all along the way.

And it's also been shown that what is often considered to be of infinite value, what is often thought to be special are often things that are less-than-perfect. Long ago in Detroit, two Rembrandt paintings were featured at a local art gallery. One of the local reviewers said that he thought one of the paintings was a fake. Experts were called to examine the paintings and it was determined that the reviewer was indeed correct. One of the paintings was not a genuine Rembrandt. When asked as to how they came to that conclusion, the experts told about how, when Rembrandt painted, there were many mistakes in his painting which he then covered up. They could see no mistakes in the one painting on display at that Detroit gallery. They deemed it too perfect to be a genuine Rembrandt.

A close examination of some of the greatest works of art will reveal imperfections which the original artist made it a point to correct, imperfections which actually served to make the painting great.

Consider if you will that valued piece of furniture which your grandfather made from an old farmhouse door. It's battered and bruised and riddled with hundreds of nicks and scratches but it's precisely those imperfections and the memories they evoke that give it the value that it has.

And how about chocolate chip cookies? Store-bought cookies are all perfect. They're evenly rounded. The chocolate chips are evenly spaced. They all look the same. Home made cookies, on the other hand, are hardly perfect at all. The number of chocolate chips will vary from cookie to cookie. They're not perfectly rounded and they can be burned at the bottom. But which, I ask you, would you prefer, which would you rather eat? Which would be a more valued addition to your cookie jars?

Great art and great furniture and great cookies are often great precisely because of their imperfections, precisely because they're anything but perfect. And, in addition to that, you'll often find that most of the greatest individuals this world has ever known could well be described as less-than-perfect.

I caught a rerun of the TV show *Bluebloods* some time ago, the cop show where Tom Selleck plays the police commissioner of New York City. A subplot had the Selleck character, Frank Ragan, being questioned by the Archbishop of New York and a Vatican official concerning a Father Bill Campion from Brooklyn who was being considered for sainthood. Ragan remembered the priest as a Vietnam War protester and there was some word that he had done something illegal, that he smuggled draft dodgers across the border of Canada. Ragan pursued it further and he came to find that the Father Bill being considered for sainthood not only had done something illegal but he also had a close relationship with a woman from his parish. When he met again with the Archbishop and the Vatican official and relayed to them that information, they seemed dismayed. Then Frank Ragan said something that moved the both of them. He told the two that if they took all the sinners out of the pool for sainthood, there wouldn't be anyone left to be a saint. Neither could argue with what he said.

It's funny, but in the quest to make Father Nelson Baker of Lackawanna a saint, I used to hear older clergy say that they couldn't make him a saint as long as his associate pastors were still alive. The point being that he wasn't the easiest guy to live with, the point being that he wasn't all that good to his associate pastors. Now that does not in any way, shape or form take away from Nelson Baker's qualifications to be a saint, but it merely provides an example of saints or 'saints to be' as people who were anything but perfect.

I remember reading of Joseph De Veuster, otherwise known as Father Damien, who worked with lepers and who was elevated to full sainthood when John Paul II was Pope. I read of how he was hygienically challenged, that he could be domineering as well as indiscreet, and he was often quite boorish. Tom Selleck's character Frank Ragan was right on target when he said if they took the sinners out of the pool for sainthood, there wouldn't be anybody left to be a saint. Saints are extraordinary men and women, but they are not perfect men and women.

And that happens to be true as well when it comes to many of the greatest individuals whoever walked the face of this earth. A member of the parish gave me a CD of Father Bill Stanton's talk on the windows here at St. Ambrose parish. It was great to hear Bill's voice again. In the talk, he spoke of someone who called him up in a rage that Martin Luther King Jr.'s picture was in one of the windows. "Don't you know that he was a womanizer?" said the caller. Bill Stanton had a great retort. He said to him: "Well, I don't know about that but there is one thing I can assure you. That's not why he's in the window!"

Cy Young the greatest pitcher who ever lived owns the record for the most wins ever 511 but he also holds the record for the most losses ever 314. Carl Ripkin holds the all-time record of having played in 2632 consecutive games. He also holds the record of most times hitting into a double play. Great people, like saints, are extraordinary men and women but they're not perfect people.

And, finally, there are the limitations which perfection tends to impose. Allan Cohen in one of his books makes a point of his wanting to be an "imperfectionist." As he saw it, a perfectionist is always seeing and finding flaws and errors that most people overlook. Though many aspects of a job may happen to have been done extremely well, a perfectionist has his or her eye on the one aspect of the job that wasn't done quite as well. So what Cohen wanted to be was an "imperfectionist" because at least he'd see and notice the beauty and the magnificence and the grandeur of all that happened to surround what happened to be less-than-perfect.

I'm reminded of Nathaniel Hawthorne's short story entitled *The Birthmark* [9]. It revolved around a man who married a beautiful woman with a small birthmark on her left cheek. She always thought it was a beauty spot but as far as her husband was concerned it spoiled her appearance. It kept her from being perfect. He became so obsessed with the birthmark that it became all that he could see. He could no longer see her beauty. He could only focus on her flaw. As a result, the woman agreed to undergo a difficult procedure to remove it. After the procedure, the birthmark faded and disappeared but the woman began to fade as well. She died shortly thereafter. That husband's obsession with perfection cost him a wife whose one imperfection never took away from her magnificent beauty.

Perfectionism can limit vision and limit satisfaction and limit love and that can cost us dearly. What Cohen wanted to be, may well be something we ought to be. As an "imperfectionist" at least we'll see and appreciate all the beauty a perfectionist will happen to miss.

Jesus in our Gospel today was taking a shot at perfection. He's telling his disciples that if it's perfection they're expecting in their ministry, they're in for a rude awakening. He's telling them to expect failure and if they experience failure, they should shake the dust from their feet and move on. Jesus was in essence readying them for the fact and reality of imperfection being embedded in ministry.

My friends, remember what is perfect may be hell. Remember, what's imperfect may be a Rembrandt. Remember, great people and great saints and great cookies are anything but perfect. And consider being an "imperfectionist.' You'll enjoy and appreciate the beauty that surrounds this less-than-perfect world in which we live.

Inclusive Not Exclusive

Matthew 15: 21-28

"...Woman, you have great faith..."

God is not small.

An exclusive interview, an exclusive resort, exclusive furniture, exclusive footwear, exclusive jewelry, an exclusive view. There is a ring of importance to the word exclusive. There is a sense of distinction whenever that word is said. If you have an exclusive, you have what very few people possess and you own what a number of people would die for. The word exclusive calls to mind prestige, status and rank, and, as such, it tends to instill a positive impression.

But as true as that is and as hallowed and as yearned for as are all things exclusive, there is its dark side. With all things exclusive, there is blindness towards a bigger and greater reality, an unwillingness to embrace a wider and a broader truth. It's that side of exclusive that I like to talk with you about today.

Let's take the church as an example. I think we've all laughed at the story of the man who went to heaven and was given a tour of the facility. As he was taken past the various sections, St. Peter pointed to various buildings and told of the people living there. But as they passed one particular building, the man was told by St. Peter to keep his voice down. When he asked why, St. Peter responded: "That's where the Catholics live and they think they're the only ones here."

I recall, when I was a boy, how I worried about all my friends who were not Catholic because I feared that they would never make it to heaven. I had been taught that the Catholic Church had the exclusive rights to the pearly gates, that no one but Catholics had access.

Not only did that smack of arrogance, but it painted a picture of God that was very small, terribly parochial, and not at all in step with the inclusive image of God found in the Scriptures. As one Native American once proclaimed: "In a tepee, the poles are separate but converge at the top. So," he said, "it is with the great spirit and the various earth travelers in search of his attention."

The idea of exclusive when it comes to God begs the truth of the vastness and the greatness and the expansiveness of God's reach. In a somewhat similar way, so it goes as well with exclusive when it comes to us. Anything exclusive when it comes to us or what we've done begs the truth of the vastness and the greatness and the expansiveness of the storehouse of knowledge and the lineage of individuals who and which happened to be on hand and at our disposal on the day we were born.

Someone complemented Thomas Edison on his originality and he replied that he happened to be a good sponge, that his ideas came from others who didn't bother to use them.

There's been a standing offer in Vienna of $25,000 to anyone who can write eight bars of original music. That offer has stood for nearly 80 years as numerous entries contained compositions that could be traced back to some other melodic creation.

It is well-known that Shakespeare was not original. He borrowed his plays from Plutarch's lives and Danish folklore and other sources. Even Lincoln's Gettysburg address has lines that can be traced to a book of sermons by Theodore Parker and those lines can be traced even further to a book on the Bible written by John Wycliffe. I can confirm that some of the angles for my sermons have come from a Dr. Bruce Thieleman whom I would later discover gleaned those angles from the works of the famed Australian preacher F.W. Boreham.

You could say that there really are no exclusive bars of music, no exclusive pieces of poetry, no exclusive designs nor exclusive ideas. So much of what we've tabbed as exclusive is and was in reality already present in the vast storehouse of knowledge from which it emerged.

And besides its origin not being exclusive, the same can be said of the finished product. I liked that story associated with Ernie Banks whom you old-timers will remember as the Hall of Fame infielder for the Chicago Cubs. Ernie had never forgotten how his father worked and sacrificed to give him a chance to play baseball. Every day, his dad left house at dawn and got back after dark. He worked so many hours that he hardly ever saw sunlight. When Ernie Banks signed his first contract with the Chicago Cubs, he sent out a three word telegram to his dad. It read: "We did it!"

Banks realized that his excellence on the baseball field was not an exclusive accomplishment, that whatever of his skills that could be tabbed exclusive were in fact a byproduct of his father's sacrifice not to mention the work of his mentors and trainers who were responsible for honing those skills.

There's nothing exclusive when it comes to achievements or accomplishments; when it comes to works of art or bars of music or pieces of poetry or whatever. They're all products of the vastness and greatness and expansiveness of the storehouse of knowledge and the lineage of individuals who and which happened to have been on hand and at our disposal on the day we were born.

Also when it comes to exclusive, there are the limitations it imposes, the narrow confines it tends to provide. In 1907, Dr. Paul Elrich discovered that the great surge of syphilis could be cured with arsenic. This was one of the first of what's been tabbed "magic bullets," a specific treatment designed to eradicate a dread disease. In the years that followed, other magic bullets were discovered. Vitamin C was found to cure scurvy and insulin replacement therapy allowed diabetics to lead a normal life. By World War II, sulfur drugs were commonly used to treat wound infections that might've been lethal in earlier times. Then there was penicillin and so many other magic bullets that gave us the idea that all illness and all disease could be treated pharmaceutically, that there was a physical cure for every physical ailment. It was then that the world of medicine began to tilt in the physical direction. It was then that an exclusive approach was adopted when it came to what ails us and what can cure us thus leaving the spiritual and emotional components of illness and recovery out of the equation. And that was to the detriment of many.

And what holds true for medicine holds true as well for other disciplines. When the physical approach becomes the exclusive approach, much is lost.

I like what Audrey Hepburn once said. Hepburn was an actress of another era and she was asked once about beauty and she gave an interesting answer. She said: "For attractive lips, speak words of kindness. For lovely eyes, seek out the good in people. For a slim figure, share your food with the hungry. For poise, walk with the knowledge that you never walk alone." It was a wonderful way of reminding people that beauty is more than skin deep, that there's more to beauty that its physical ingredients.

I'm reminded of that poignant scene from Chaim Potok's celebrated novel *The Chosen*[10]. A father complains to his neighbors of his son's brilliance calling it a curse instead of a blessing. "My God, my God, what are you doing to me?" he cried. "A mind like this I need for a son? A heart I need for a son, compassion I want for my son. Righteousness, mercy, the strength to suffer and carry pain, that's what I want from my son, not a mind without a soul."

When it comes to exclusive, there is a dimension omitted, a component expunged, an ingredient left out. Whether it be medicine or beauty or character or whatever, there are many parts to the whole, many shades to the picture, many variations to the music, and many elements to the diagnosis. There's more to illness than a physical problem, more to beauty than a gorgeous figure, more to a person than a brilliant mind. When it comes to exclusive, there are the limitations it imposes, the narrow confines it tends to provide.

And, finally, when it comes to exclusive, there is a superiority and exclusion it often happens to imply. I recall here a conversation Archie Bunker had with his black neighbor George Jefferson. It had to do with God. Archie, with his typically limited mindset, presumed George to be an atheist only to be told by George that he did believe in God. "Well," said Archie, "it's interesting how the black people went from worshiping snakes and beads and wooden idols all the way up to our God" "What do you mean 'your God?'" replied George only to have Archie tell him that he's a white man's God. "What makes you think God isn't black?" asked George. And the bigoted Bunker tells him: "It's because God created man in his own image and you will note," said Archie, "I ain't black."

Whether it be racism, sexism, ageism or any of the isms, there's this sense of superiority surrounding it. There is a sense of exclusion sitting at its heart. All too often people like an Archie Bunker believe that when it comes to the human race, they are part of an exclusive club and left out is anyone or anything that does not possess the particulars of the race, the age, or the gender to which they happen to subscribe. When it comes to exclusive, there's this dark side, there are its many negative implications.

In looking at today's Gospel, in particular the exchange between Jesus and the Canaanite woman, we're given the impression that when it comes to God, inclusive is in and exclusive is out, that God is a big God not a small God, that God is not into putting limits on the extent of his love.

Implicit in that truth is a call to quit the idea that only Catholics and Christians make it to heaven. Implicit in that truth is the call to quit this idea that we were responsible for an exclusive creation, this idea that we did what we did all by our lonesome. Implicit in that truth is a call to quit the notion that beauty is only skin deep or that medicine has to do with magic bullets. Implicit in that truth is the call to quit the notion that our age or our race or our gender puts us a step above the rest.

God is calling us today to think inclusive and not exclusive, to not think or believe small, but to think and believe large; to embrace a much broader, much wider view when it comes to life and when it comes to us.

I close with a piece of poetry by Edwin Markham. "They drew a circle that shut me out: heretic, rebel, a thing to flout. But love and I had the wit to win; we drew a circle that took them in."

Life Expectancy

Mark 13: 33-37

"...You do not know when the appointed time will come..."

Death often arrives much sooner than expected.

A study of nature reveals that various life forms have different life expectancies. A mouse can expect to live 4 years, a rabbit 9 years, a pigeon 26, a deer 35, a crocodile 40, and an elephant can expect to live 70 years. The oldest chimpanzee, Cheetah, is 74 and, yes, he's the same Cheetah that starred in those Tarzan movies of long ago. Bowhead whales have been found with harpoons in their bodies dating back to the eighteen hundreds, one such whale, after an autopsy, was determined to be 211years of age. And then there are the Aldabra tortoises, one of whom died in 2006 at the age of 255.

Similar variables of life expectancy can be found in the plant and insect kingdoms. A certain bristlecone pine tree, appropriately called Methuselah, lives somewhere in the white mountains of California. Scientists say it is 4,770 years old, the oldest living single organism ever documented. On the shorter end of the scale sits the worker bee who lives only one year, the worker ant who lives but a half a year, and some species of moths who live for a mere 24 hours.

And then when it comes to the human race, life expectancy varies from country to country. An American can expect to live 77.7 years while a Mozambican has a life expectancy of a mere 40.3 years. Spain has the highest life expectancy of 82.3 years while those living in third world countries often do even worse than Mozambicans when it comes to the years its citizens are expected to live. The oldest documented human being was Jeanne Calmet of Arles, France who lived to 122 years and 164 days of age.

Life Injections IV

I have taken you on a very lengthy but hopefully interesting walk down life expectancy lane because we happen to be nearing the end of another year. In a few short weeks, it could well be said that we have one less year to live. And as our Scriptures for this time of the year so frequently tell us, there are no guarantees when it comes to life expectancy. There are no assurances that we're going to realize all the years that we are expected to live. As today's Gospel so well states, we do not know when the Lord of the house is coming. We do not know when our time is up as far as the living of our life is concerned.

So what I'd like to talk with you about is not putting off what we should be doing today. I'd like to discuss with you the matter of making sure we have our house in order. The truth is, the fact is, that the Lord of the house may decide to come calling much sooner than we had hoped or expected.

Stephen Levine, the famed therapist, once asked his audience that if they had one hour to live and they could make one phone call, who would it be to and what would they say. And then he threw out the zinger. "What are you waiting for? Make the call now?"

That Steven Levine question played out in real life some years back. I am referring to those on an airplane and at the World Trade Center on that fateful 9/11 day. The people knew they were facing certain death and they did indeed make calls and they weren't to their stockbrokers, they weren't to their bosses back at the home office. They called the ones they loved telling them of their love and telling them how much they appreciated their years together.

If there are people in our life whom we really care about, if there are people in our life whom we really love, we need to tell them. We need to let them know how much we appreciate them. And we need to do it now! Unbeknownst to us, the Lord of the house may be coming very soon and chances are that, unlike those folks on that airplane or in the World Trade Center on September 11th, last minute phone calls will not be an option. And wouldn't it be a terrible shame if we went to our graves and our loved ones went to theirs without any known record of our saying one word about how much we had loved and appreciated them.

And wouldn't it be a shame if we got to our graves without having mended our fences, without having resolved a dispute it would've done us well to resolve. I'm reminded of a tale from the Civil War involving a general and one of the men under his command. The general was dying in a log cabin and so wished to reconcile with a soldier he had wrongly punished. His only words were "Find, Imboden!" that was the soldier's name. All through the night, the general's men scoured the woods and fields and roads looking for Imboden. At long last, they found him and brought him to the dying general's cabin telling him of the general's fate and telling him as well that the feud between them was unfounded, that it was all a misunderstanding. Filled with regret, filled with remorse, Imboden came to the general's side and called him by name and with tears in his eyes, he said: "I am sorry." But it was too late, the general was dead, his dying wish never granted and Imboden would go to his grave filled with remorse.

You might recall my telling you of a high school graduate who left home in disgust and anger because his father never bought him the car he promised him as a graduation gift and gave him, instead, a Bible, a Bible which he promptly threw to the floor in disgust upon receiving it. As it happened, he never spoke to his father again. When his father died, he felt it his duty to attend the funeral and so he did. Afterwards, he went back to his father's home and looking through his belongings discovers the Bible he had thrown to the floor. When he opened the Bible, he saw taped to the page a cashier's check for that car he had hoped to receive dated the day of his graduation.

Stupid things happen. Misunderstandings are common. Stories get mixed up. Facts aren't always what they're thought to be. Not knowing the time or the hour of our death and with a life expectancy of no guarantees, we mustn't wait on reconciliation. We mustn't let a dispute simmer because it could well be that we had it all wrong, that we didn't have our facts straight and how sad it would be if we went to our graves not having realized that truth. And even if the facts were straight and we didn't have it wrong, how sad it would be that we went to our graves as someone who was too stubborn or too self righteous to have made a move towards reconciliation.

And then when it comes to our questionable life expectancies, there's the matter of our legacy. In one of those English detective stories where everyone is under suspicion for murder from the butler to the Archbishop of Canterbury, a disgruntled detective said: "This was the perfect crime. The guilty party never left a fingerprint anywhere."

What no one should ever do is commit the perfect crime when it comes to life, the perfect crime being the failure to leave a fingerprint anywhere, the failure to leave a mark on an institution or cause or person greater than oneself.

Some years ago, I had to officiate at back to back funerals at two different churches. One man was a doctor and the other worked in a flour mill. At face value, it seemed the doctor had it all over the mill worker in terms of a life lived. He made a lot more money, he had a lot more prestige, and he lived better in terms of the finer things of life. It proved to be a false assumption.

What I do whenever I conduct a funeral is spend time with the deceased's family and friends usually with pen and paper in hand hoping to jot down stories and anecdotes and qualities and characteristics of the one who had passed away. I then use the material to forge my homily. When I interviewed friends and family of the doctor, I was not able to jot down a word. I didn't put down a single note on the pad of paper I had brought for the interview. It was because the family couldn't tell me anything about him. It was obvious that he hadn't made an impact on anyone's life. And as far as that mill worker was concerned, I left my interview with his family and friends with tons of notes. I could've talked about him for hours.

What had happened was that the doctor had committed the perfect crime. He didn't leave a fingerprint anywhere. The mill worker in contrast had his fingerprints on many people's lives as well as many causes and institutions of which he played a part.

Since we're not sure we're going to achieve our life expectancies, since there are no guarantees when it comes to our length of stay in this world, it would behoove us to take a look at the conduct of our lives to see if we're leaving our fingerprints anywhere. It would be a real shame if our life would suddenly come to an end and it did so with our committing the perfect crime against life, no legacy to speak of.

And then finally when it comes to our questionable life expectancies, there's the matter of our destiny. I always liked that Mark Twain story in which a man died and met Saint Peter at the pearly gates. Realizing that Saint Peter was a wise and knowledgeable individual, the man shared with him his interest in military history and inquired of him as to who was the greatest General of all time. Saint Peter quickly replied: "That's easy; it's that fellow over there!" "You must be mistaken," said the man, "I know that individual. He lived near where I lived and he was a common laborer and was a private in the army." "That is correct, my friend," said Saint Peter, "but had he exercised his potential, he'd have been the greatest General that ever lived."

Cartoonist Charles Schultz once said that life is like a ten speed bike and it is a shame as to how many fail to use all the gears. God has gifted us all with multiple talents which he fully expects us to use. We may be a General in the making, we may be a musician in the making, and we may be a great person in the making. It comes down to a matter of using all the gears on our bicycles. It comes down to a matter of exercising our potentials and would it not be a real shame if our life expectancy gets unexpectedly shortened and we end up like that would be general in Mark Twain's story, entering our grave without realizing our destiny.

There's an old poem that speaks of the length of one's life in a unique way. It describes how the dates on a tombstone are often separated by a dash. The poet muses that the dash represents all the time the person lived on earth and then remarked as to how we never know how short or long our dash will be. What matters in the end, he says, are not the dates on the tombstone but what matters is how we've lived our dash.

My friends, it would be nice if we can all reach our life expectancy of 77.7 years but as you and I know, it may not happen and in fact it might be that we're going to reach the second date on our tombstones a lot sooner than expected. So it behooves us to let the people we love know we love them. It behooves us to settle all disputes and misunderstandings that may still be simmering. It behooves us to start caring about someone or something other than ourselves so that upon our deaths it won't be said of us that we committed the perfect crime. It behooves us to start engaging all the gears on our bicycles so there won't be the lament that we could've been what we weren't.

If we do what it behooves us to do and we die before our life expectancy is achieved, then that dash on our tombstone will be free of any shame or remorse or lament. That dash on our tombstone will speak of a life well lived and a life well loved.

The Invitation to Live

Mark 16: 1-7

"...He has been raised, he is not here..."

Life often presents us with a set of invitations, one to live and one to die.

If you were to ask me as to what was the best article I ever read, I'd immediately cite an article that appeared in a nursing journal in the early seventies. It was written by Doctor Sidney Jouard and it was entitled *The Invitation to Die*. In that article, Dr. Jouard posited the fact that periodically in the course of life, something will happen, something will be experienced, some event will take place that will strike at the very core of the meaning and the purpose of that life and the person will interpret it to be an invitation to die. And all too often the invitation is accepted and that person will end their life either by an overt act of suicide or by consuming drugs or alcohol over an extended period of time or will do so through some activity or non-activity that is sure to result in a life that will end before its time.

I bring that Sidney Jouard article to your attention this Easter morning because I believe that in rising to new life Jesus provides a counteroffer to that invitation to die, that if in fact you had something happen or have experienced something or have had something take place that has struck at the very core of the meaning and the purpose of your life, Jesus invites you to live, Jesus presents an alternative to death and that alternative is new life.

I call to your attention a man named W. Mitchell who in 1971 was horribly burned and nearly killed and left fingerless from a freak motorcycle accident. Sixteen surgeries were required resulting in an inability to pick up a fork or dial a telephone or attend to basic

Life Injections IV

hygienic needs. Mitchell was determined, however, not to let those handicaps deter him from living. It wasn't long thereafter that he teamed up with two friends and founded a wood burning stove company which became Vermont's second largest employer.

In the midst of all of that success, tragedy would strike Mitchell yet another time. The plane he was piloting crashed onto the runway during a takeoff crushing Mitchell's twelve thoracic vertebrae and permanently paralyzing him from the waist down. Undaunted yet again, he worked night and day to regain as much independence as possible. He was soon thereafter elected Mayor of Crest Bluff, Colorado. He began whitewater rafting. He fell in love and got married and earned a master's degree in public administration. He now tours the country giving motivational speeches.

Now admittedly we're talking here about an extraordinary individual but W. Mitchell is an example of someone who received not one but two invitations to die and he chose to tear up the invitation and to accept instead Christ's invitation to live. He could have sulked and been bitter and angry. He could've taken to anesthetizing his misery with alcohol or drugs. Instead he made good on the opportunities that his troubles afforded him. He entered upon new life.

Alfred Adler, the famed psychologist, once told of two men each of whom lost an arm. At the end of a year, one had grown so discouraged by his handicap that he decided that life was no longer worth living. The other was so triumphant that he went about saying that he really did not know why nature had given him two arms when he could get along perfectly well with one. A parallel tragedy was had; one accepted the invitation to die while the other accepted the invitation to live.

I'm reminded of a similar parallel involving the breakup of a relationship. Two men got jilted by the woman they loved. One left a note on the Henley Street Bridge in a town near Tennessee saying that the only girl he ever loved is gone and he can't live without her and he leaped from the bridge to his death. The other young man decided to write a song expressing his misery and heartache. It engendered $20,000 in royalties and helped him land a new career as a singer. Sorrow and rejection struck two men. One accepted the invitation to die while the other tore it up and accepted instead the invitation to live.

And so it goes so often in life. The script is an all too familiar one. Everything is going along perfectly well. Everything seems to be falling neatly into place and then suddenly a tragedy strikes, a problem occurs, a loss is realized, some bad things happens and, in the face of it, there is a set of invitations given, to live or to die, and how we choose makes all the difference in the world.

On the night of December 9, 1914, the great Edison Industries of West Orange, New Jersey was virtually destroyed by a fire. Thomas Edison lost $2 million that night as much of his life's work went up in flames. Edison was 67 years old at the time. The next morning, walking amidst the charred embers of all he had worked for, Thomas Edison says to his son: "Charlie, there is great value in disasters. All our mistakes are burned up. Thank God, we can start anew." Three weeks after the fire, Edison industries delivered its first phonograph.

The invitation to die rested in those burning embers of West Orange, New Jersey. It would have been logical for Thomas Edison to accept it. After all, he was already an accomplished inventor. He made his mark on history. He was 67 years of age. But he wouldn't accept the invitation. He chose instead to accept the invitation to live and he rebuilt his factory and rebuilt his life.

So be it a handicap, be it a loss of a loved one, be it a fire, an earthquake, or a natural disaster, when the train of life gets derailed, when all that we had going for us ends up in flames, when we're faced with the fact that life as we know it will never be the same again, we can choose to accept the invitation to live or we can choose to accept the invitation to die. We can stay in the tomb which life has put us in or we can exit through the door marked "new life". The choice is ours.

Edward Arlington Robinson once wrote a poem that Simon and Garfunkel put into song. It was a poem about Richard Cory, the man who had everything: wealth, fame, notoriety. He had all that a person could ever hope to have. The irony was that although he had everything, he was never satisfied and one night he came home and put a bullet in his head.

One would think that wealth carries with it an invitation to live since the worries and struggles for financial security have come to an end. But all too often, there's another invitation that's received as well and that's the invitation to rest on one's laurels, to sit back on one's accomplishments, to wallow in the emptiness of a life without any demands or challenges or possibilities, in essence an invitation to die. And down through the years, we've seen that invitation get accepted in Richard Cory fashion and sometimes we've seen it accepted over the long haul via self destructive habits not unlike those chronicled in tabloids next to cash resisters in the supermarket nearest you.

Be it wealth, be it retirement or be it any of the luxuries and advantages that come life's way, you're also presented with the invitation to live and the invitation to die. Those invitations, you see, come not only when bad things happen but they come when good things happen as well.

Some 2000 years ago, Jesus appeared on this day to his apostles to bring home the message that new life can be found in the midst of death, that death needn't be accepted as the final word, that from death can come forth new life.

So, my friends, if you've met with tragedy or you've met with luxury; if you've experienced a loss or you've experienced a gain: if you've made a mistake or you've achieved a success; if a bad thing has happened to you or a good thing has happened to you. You can choose to be bitter or you can choose to be better. You can choose to quit living or you can choose to start living. You can choose to be empty or you can choose to be full. You can choose to be remorseful or you can choose to be resourceful. You can choose to accept the invitation to live or you can choose to accept the invitation to die.

Be an Easter people! Should you find yourself in a tomb, exit out that door that Jesus built, the door marked new life. Choose the invitation to live!

Nothing Matters

1 Corinthians 1: 26-31

"...God chose...those who count for nothing..."

What may be written off as nothing may in fact be something.

When TV Guide did its ranking of the 50th greatest shows of all time, it gave its number one ranking to the show known as Seinfeld. I believe we are all familiar with the sitcom. Jerry Seinfeld, George Costanza, Elaine Benes, and Kramer are the characters and each week you would find them at the corner coffee shop or at a Chinese restaurant or a movie theater or a mall parking lot and they'd engage in a conversation the contents of which would often be discussed around water coolers in offices all across the country. If pressed to describe the show, its creator would tell you that it was a show about nothing.

Well, it's "nothing" that I'd like to talk with you about today. It's "nothing" I'd like to discuss with you today. Just as the Seinfeld show about nothing was really something, so can it be that what is perceived to be nothing is really something, so can it be where "nothing" has been anything but nothing.

There's an old whimsical tale where a coal mouse asked a wild dove: "Tell me the weight of a snowflake!" And the dove responded: "Nothing more than nothing!" "In that case," said the coal mouse, "let me tell you a marvelous story. I sat on a Christmas tree branch close to the trunk when it began to snow. Not heavily, not a raging blizzard; you might say it snowed one flake at a time. Having nothing better to do, I counted the snowflakes settling on the twigs and needles of my branch. Their number was exactly 3,471,902. When the next snowflake dropped onto the branch, 'nothing more than nothing' as you say, the branch broke off."

Life Injections IV

Completing the story, the coal mouse fled leaving the dove to ponder what was said. The dove, since Noah's time, an authority on the matter said to herself: "Perhaps, there is one voice lacking for peace to come to the world."

That whimsical tale is more truth than fiction as time and again one small deed, nothing more than nothing as we might describe it, one small deed has proven to be a powerful force behind some monumental change, some extraordinary turnaround, and some remarkable event. I've known where a single smile had kept a young man from suicide. I read where one word kept a famous author from giving up his trade. I saw in Boys Life where a tiny tin of aspirin sent by a young scout translated into a quarter of a million dollars getting donated to a mission in Africa. And it was reported where one letter of complaint resulted in a multi-national corporation calling a halt to its assault upon the environment.

On more than a few occasions, nothing has proven to be something. On more than a few occasions, what could well be dismissed as nothing has proven to be anything but nothing. It made an impact no one would have ever conceived as possible.

And when it comes to nothing, there's the matter of restraint. F.W. Boreham tells of Alfred Russell Wallace coming upon an Emperor moth beating its wings and struggling wildly to force its passage through the narrow neck of its cocoon. He admired his fine proportions, 8 inches from the top of one wing to the top of the other, and thought it a pity that so handsome a creature should be subjected to so severe a trial. He, therefore, took out his pen knife and slit the cocoon. The moth came out at once but its glorious colors never developed, the soaring wings never expanded. The indescribable hues and tints and shades that usually adorned those wings never did appear. The moth lived but a short time and died. The furious struggle with the cocoon was nature's wise way of developing the moth's splendid wings. It was nature's wise way of sending the vital fluids pulsing through the moth's body so every particular organ and source of beauty could be fully developed. Alfred Russell Wallace had saved the little creature from the struggle but had unintentionally ruined and slain it in the process.

What Wallace learned was a lesson parents often fail to learn and that's the importance of restraint, the importance of doing nothing when every fiber of one's being wants to do something. In a child's struggle with life, there are times when a parent needs to do something but there are times when a parent needs to do nothing and the latter is far more difficult than the former. Call it tough love, call it restraint; a child's development, a child's true calling, a child's future will often rest on our doing nothing rather than the something we so want to do.

Also when it comes to nothing being something, there's the matter of ministry. On more than a few occasions, I've been touched by someone coming up to me and thanking me profusely for all the help I provided them when their loved one passed away at Sisters Hospital. In most of those cases, I really didn't do anything, I did nothing except be there with them during that trying time in their life.

I've come to learn through the years that the best ministry we can provide someone at a time of tragedy is the ministry of doing nothing because the something of mouthing empty and painful clichés; the something of sending flowers and casseroles; the something of giving a rationale for the tragedy or far worse comparing it to one's own difficult times; those somethings cannot substitute for our quiet presence. Those somethings cannot substitute for standing by and doing nothing except to exude the love and the compassion their pain has called forth from inside us.

I can't help but recall here the story involving one of the great churchmen of the previous century Henry Drummond. A woman whose husband was dying came to Drummond one late Saturday evening and begged him to come to her home. "My husband is dying, sir!" she said. "He's not able to speak to you and is unable to hear you but please do come to see him!" "But ma'am," said Drummond, "if your husband can't hear nor speak, it's no use of my coming." At which point the woman pleaded; "Oh do come please! I'd give anything for my husband to have a breath of you before he dies."

More times than not, just a breath of us is all someone needs to be ministered to, 'nothing more than nothing' as that dove would have described it. But, Oh! How powerful that breath can be when there is love in the heart of the one doing the breathing.

Besides nothing, at times, being ministry, so can nothing, at times, be life saving. Dr. Larry Dossey wrote a piece in one of his books of a member of an expedition force in Antarctica. He lost his way under blizzard conditions and found himself buried in snow. He realized that to do anything would only exhaust him and probably hasten his death. So he chose not to do anything, to act, in his words, 'like a baby in a womb." When morning came, he heard someone call his name and he emerged from his snow burial alive and well.

Common practice for nomadic Arabs is to do nothing when a sandstorm overtakes their ride through the desert. He'll dismount his camel, lie down upon the sand and cover his head and quietly wait for the storm to pass. Pilots were trained during World War II to do nothing when the plane took on enemy fire because immediate reactions would often prompt disastrous decisions.

Doing nothing buys time, time to think, time to ponder, time to make sure that the next step that's taken is the right step and not one fraught with catastrophic consequences. Doing nothing can spare us from any regrets over the direction our instincts might have possibly taken us. It could well be said that nothing can have lifesaving qualities.

Then there's the fact of nothing proving to be something in and of itself. A black baby was born to a slave mother near Diamond Grove, Missouri just as the Civil War was coming to an end. One night, the infant and his mother were stolen by night riders and taken to Arkansas. The owner hired John Bentley to find the baby and his mother and bring them back to Missouri. When Bentley returned several days later, he brought back only the baby and he was close to death.

When the Master asked Bentley as to how it was he could find the baby and not the mother, Bentley replied that the night riders had kept the mother because she was valuable and as hard as he tried he could not detect their trail. As far as the baby was concerned, the night riders determined him to be of no value and they passed him on to some womenfolk whom they happened to have encountered along the way. The baby who was worth nothing was George Washington Carver who grew up to be one of the greatest scientists the South ever produced.

You may recall my telling you of a famous cartoon that showed two Kentucky backwoodsmen standing in the snow at the edge of a forest. One asked the other: "Anything new?" The other replied: "Nothing!" Then by way of an afterthought he says: "there was a baby born over at Tom Lincoln's log cabin last night. But be rest assured, nothing ever happens around here."

What often passes for nothing, what's often said to be worth nothing, can not only prove to be something but it can prove to be something wonderful, something great, something fantastic. God has made it clear that no one is a nothing, that we are in fact God's sons and daughters, brothers and sisters to Christ. When it comes to what's perceived as nothing, more times than not it's anything but nothing.

And, finally, when it comes to nothing, there's the matter of beauty. Some years back, the White House fell into the hands of painters and decorators. Two large exterior doors had been painted to represent black walnut and the contractor ordered his men to scrape and clean them in readiness for a fresh coat of paint. But when the scrapers penetrated to the solid timber below the paint, they discovered to their astonishment that it was mahogany wood with this most exquisite natural grain. The earlier decorators thought they were adding to the beauty of the timber with a coat of paint, but instead what they did was conceal its essential and inherent glory.

All too often, a beautiful face, a beautiful piece of wood, a beautiful piece of scenery is beautiful in and of itself. Its beauty is best served by doing nothing, best served by not doing anything because anything would mar its essential and inherent glory.

In our second reading today, Paul writes: "God chose those who count for nothing to reduce to nothing those who are something." You might say he was telling the Corinthians that "nothing" matters.

It matters in that it can be that 3 millionth snowflake that breaks the branch, the smile that can save a person's life. "Nothing" matters in that it can be pregnant with possibilities, that what's labeled as nothing may indeed be something like a future President of the United States. "Nothing" matters in that it can be a ministry, a ministry of standing by and doing nothing but being present for the one who hurts. "Nothing" matters in that it kept paint and makeup and clutter from marring what is naturally and essentially beautiful. "Nothing" matters in that it buys time so that disastrous mistakes will not be made. "Nothing" matters in that a beautiful butterfly to be will not be robbed of the struggle necessary for its beauty to unfold.

The Seinfeld show was about nothing and it proved to be really something. St. Paul reminds us today that what may be written off as nothing may well indeed prove to be really something.

Surprise

Luke 1: 39-45

"...But who am I that the mother of my Lord should come to me..."

God's mode of operation has often been a surprise.

The defendant was on trial for murder. There was strong evidence indicating his guilt, but there was no body, no corpus to seal the deal. In his closing argument, the defense attorney announced: "Ladies and gentlemen of the jury! I have a big surprise for you. Within one minute, the man presumed to be dead is going to walk through those courtroom doors." All the eyes of the jury were glued to those doors. A minute passed, another minute passed. The surprise did not occur. No one entered the courtroom. The defense attorney then announced: "Ladies and gentlemen of the jury! Since all of you anticipated that the man presumed to be dead was going to walk through those courtroom doors, you have no choice but to render a not guilty verdict because there is reasonable doubt that the victim ever died or was killed.

The jury retired to deliberate. A few minutes later, they returned and pronounced a verdict of guilty. The defense attorney was dumbfounded. "How could you render that decision?" He cried. "Surely, you must have had doubts! You all stared at the door!" The jury foreman replied: "Yes, we stared at the door, but your client did not!"

It's surprise that I'd like to talk with you about today. Not surprise as a ploy to fool a jury, but surprise as a means for God's glory, surprise as a sign of God interacting with the world around us. There are many blessings, many revelations, many moving moments, many awakenings that have come our way thanks to the element of surprise.

Life Injections IV

William Roentgen was working to improve some photographic equipment. As he leaned the wrong way on the table, a fluorescent like flash occurred. That surprise development would lead him down a track that ultimately bred the x-ray machine.

Duane Pearsall was testing an electronic device that controlled static electricity. And it happened that smoke from a technician's cigarette short-circuited its meter. That surprise occurrence led him down a path that ultimately gave birth to the smoke alarm otherwise known as the smoke detector and that device has saved tens of thousands of lives.

And, of course, we are all familiar with the story of Sir Alexander Fleming who had been conducting experiments on bacteria in his laboratory in London. A breeze from an open window fell upon the Petri dishes and particles of mold began eating away at the bacteria. That surprise occurrence would lead to the discovery of penicillin, a Nobel Prize for Fleming, and the conquering of diseases for which previously there was no cure.

The element of surprise has been responsible for countless numbers of discoveries and medicines and inventions that have made our lives easier, made them safer, and have been responsible for the eradication of many ailments and maladies which had previously claimed innumerable lives and many a livelihood. And who's to say in light of it all that it wasn't God who was responsible for the surprise.

And how about God's surprise appearances? How about the fact that God's presence has been found in the most unusual of places and in the most unlikely of individuals? I always liked that Christmas story where Conrad the Cobbler was told in a vision that God was going to visit him the next day. The next day comes and Conrad is filled with tremendous anticipation. As he waits by the store, he notices a mother and her family in distress and he ministers to them. And then there is a beggar that comes by who is freezing from the cold and the Cobbler provides him with his coat. Someone else passes by who's in need of food and he feeds them. The day ends and there was no sign of God. Terribly disappointed, Conrad the Cobbler goes to bed only to discover in a dream that God did indeed visit him that day but surprised him by donning the disguise of that mother and that beggar and that person in need.

And then how about the true story involving St. Francis of Assisi. The man always had a terrible aversion to the disease of leprosy and could hardly bring himself to even look at a person so afflicted. One day as he was riding along, he's suddenly confronted by a leper who cried out for help. Francis's first reaction was one of utter repulsion. But then with an act of courage even greater than a soldier's daring in battle, he dismounted and embraced the pitiful creature. As he did this, he got his first glimpse of the leper's face and, according to the story, what he saw was the countenance of Christ himself.

And consider if you will Richard Carlson who met a waitress in a restaurant who had been through a painful experience similar to his own and, thanks to that conversation, he joined a church and gained a whole new group of friends. Carlson said he could trace his entire healing process back to that waitress whom he had never seen again.

The waitress, the leper, the beggar, the person in need, the woman in distress are all examples of God's surprise appearances, all demonstrative of God choosing to make his presence felt in a surprising way.

And besides surprise being a cover for God's presence, surprise is also at the center of Christ's teachings. Many a parable is revelatory of a God who operates in surprising ways.

A colleague of mine once told of how one day when he was a young child he was particularly naughty. He was sent to his bed by his mother with the warning of a punishment that would be forthcoming once his dad returned home. He said he shivered in his bed in fright and his fear became acute as he heard his father's key turning the latch on the front door. He decided not to wait in his room to receive his punishment and so he descended down the stairs to meet his dad. He had gotten down a few steps when his father sketched out his arms and cried out: "My dear, wee son!" The hug and the embrace was not the punishment he expected. To this day, tears well up in his eyes when he retells the story.

It's not the prodigal son story but it certainly contained its elements. My colleague was surprised as to his dad's reaction to his misdeed just as the prodigal son was surprised as to his father's reaction to his misdeed. And when you think of it, the whole concept of a forgiving God is a big surprise to all of us because not only do we expect punishment but we'd be the first to deliver it if someone ever crossed us, if someone ever violated our trust.

Perhaps that explains the results of a recent survey where many said that they'd given up the faith not because it was too hard to believe but because it was too good to believe. The more you read the parables of Jesus, the more you're surprised at the goodness of God, the more you're surprised that God would be as understanding as forgiving and as caring as the parables make him out to be.

And not only is there surprise in God's temperament, but there is also surprise in God's power. I like the fable of the piece of iron. Many attempts were made to break it but they were met with failure. "I'll break it!" said the axe and his blows fell heavily upon the piece of iron but every blow made the axe's edge more blunt until it finally ceased to strike the iron. It gave up in frustration. "Leave it to me!" said the saw, and it worked back and forth on the iron surface until its jagged teeth were all worn and broken. Then in despair, the saw quit trying and fell to the side. "Ah!" said the hammer. "I knew you two wouldn't succeed. I'll show you how to do it." But at the first fierce blow, off flew the head of the hammer and the piece of iron remained just as it was before: proud and hard and unchanged. "Let me try!" said the small soft flame and the offer was met with doubt and cynicism. No one believed something that small could perform so powerful a fete. But the small soft flame curled around the piece of iron and embraced it and never left it until the iron melted into a powerless pool of liquid.

I'm reminded of the contest between the seed and a great rock. No one gave the seed a chance but over the years the seed's tendrils began penetrating the rock's crevices and, in the course of its growth, it tore the rock in two. That seed and that flame demonstrated God's surprising power.

Think of Gandhi freeing India from the coercive grip of British rule. Think of Rosa Parks taking a seat on the bus and turning the tide on hundreds of years of segregation. Think of Nelson Mandela leaving prison where he spent 25 years of his life and then he subsequently upended an apartheid system a worldwide boycott could not end. It's been small flames and tiny seeds like Mandela and Rosa Parks and Gandhi who have flexed God's muscle and melted down and cracked entrenched systems of evil which far more powerful forces were not able to put to an end.

And, finally, when it comes to the element of surprise, there is the matter of nature. When some people think of Death Valley National Park, they think of an oppressive, hot and arid desert that can barely support any life. In 2005, something beautiful and extraordinary happened. The arid desert received in a short span of time 6 inches of rain, an amount unheard of in Death Valley's history. Visitors to the park at that time had a glorious surprise. The abundant rainfall caused dormant seeds to germinate into exquisite purple, yellow and other boldly colored desert flowers, one of which had delicate orchid like leaves which unfolded into a flower which could take your breath away. God will often use the element of surprise in nature to fill us with awe, to dazzle us with wonder.

I reference the element of surprise today because first of all that's what Christmas is all about, the surprising news that God who could've washed his hands of us instead decided to move in and share with us his life. And I reference the element of surprise as well because our Gospel highlights the surprising news that Zachariah and Elizabeth, a childless and old couple, have conceived a child, a child who would prepare the way of the Lord. Surprise, you might say is God's mode of operation. It's how God communicates with his people.

He communicates his concern for our welfare by surprising Roentgen with a flashing light and Fleming with mold in his Petri dish. God communicates his presence through the surprising disguises of a beggar and a leper. God communicates his power through the surprising seeds and flames known as Gandhi, Mandela and Parks. God communicates awe and wonder through the surprising antics of nature. God communicates good news through the surprising parables that speak of things too good to fathom as truth. My friends, whenever you are surprised, think of God. It's his mode of operation.

Is There Any Hope

Isaiah 35: 1-6, 10

"...Then will the eyes of the blind be opened..."

Why we should be hopeful.

I read of a submarine which sank in the Atlantic Ocean during the Second World War. A team was sent down to that sub in a diving bell to see if somehow the trapped crew might be saved. When the bell settled against the sub, the trapped crew was able to communicate with the world outside for the first time since the sinking occurred. Tapping in Morse code against the connecting steel, the men in the sub asked their fateful question: "Is there any hope?"

"Is there any hope?" is a question many of us have as we look at the world around us. There are so many bad things happening. There are so many ideals and moral principles that seem to be eroding. There's so much perversity at work in our world that it is difficult to see anything we can be hopeful about. That being the case, and Advent being the season of hope, I thought I'd talk with you about why we should be hopeful. Why it is that even though things look bad, we should never give up hope.

First of all, things have looked bad before. I came across an editorial that read as to how this is the gloomiest moment in the history of the United States. Not in any one's lifetime has there been so much grave and deep apprehension. The domestic economic situation is in shambles. Trouble across the land continues to multiply. The future appears awfully grim. That editorial appeared in Harper's Weekly in October of 1837. I remember reading a similar piece decrying the loss of values and the lack of discipline and the despicable behavior of our youth.

And that piece came from an archaeological dig that dated back to the days of Julius Caesar.

As bad as things appear to be today, there have been times in human history when things were bad as well, many times in human history when things were in fact a whole lot worse. We survived the bad before and so we can be hopeful that we will survive the bad once again. And when you consider how the media accentuates the negative, how it's before our eyes much more so than it's ever been before, it may well be that things really aren't as bad as we think. That in fact we might actually be living in a much better and more hopeful time than may appear to be the case from the watching of the evening news.

The second reason we should be hopeful, the second reason why we should never give up hope can be summed up in that phrase made famous by the New York State lottery: "Hey, you never know!"

I reference the story of the Jewish man who was preparing for the approach of the high holy days. An acquaintance asked why he was going to go through the routine of repentance for all of his sins if, year after year, he only commits them all over again. The man replied saying "You're right! From year to year I repent and succumb to many of the same sins of which I've repented. But each year I believe that maybe this will be the year that I change.

Who is to say that this won't be the year that people change, that this won't be the year that things take a turn for the better. Who's to say that this won't be the year that peace will come to some war torn country that reconciliation will come to a relationship that's been torn asunder, that an end will come to an injustice that's been entrenched for many long years. Who's to say that there aren't things happening in some corner of the world that will in the very near future have a tremendously positive impact upon the world? It may not appear that things are ever going to change but maybe, as that Jewish fellow believed, maybe this will be the year that things will change and we will see something wonderful take place that so many had thought to be far beyond the realm of possibility.

The third reason why we should be hopeful, the third reason why we should never give up hope is that it sure beats the alternative. I recently read a book by Paul Pearsall entitled The Beethoven Factor[11] and he tells of a client named Patsy who was one of the most hopeful patients he had ever met. Patsy was well loved throughout the cancer ward of the hospital because of her upbeat nature and because she was such a positive influence on so many of the patients who encountered her. Unfortunately, despite all of her hope, Patsy died right on schedule. She lived barely a day beyond the time allotted for her particular cancer. At the time of her death, her parents heard a medical resident say in disgust: "A lot of good her hope did her."

The parents went up to the resident and told him point blank that hope did everything for Patsy. "I'll have you know," they said, "that hope was the energy that kept her going upward even though her cancer was dragging her downward. Hope was the energy that made these past two weeks a positive time for her as well as for us, her family. You see, Doctor, hope doesn't guarantee you won't die. It only guarantees that you can enjoy living." The alternative to hope is despair and, if we choose despair over hope, whatever living we might have left to live will be lived in misery and sadness and discontent.

I'm reminded of two young brothers who went to their backyard one day to dig a hole to China. They dug and dug and dug. Sometime thereafter an older kid walked by and asked what they were doing. "We're digging a hole to China," they told him. The older kid laughed and laughed and said: "You fools! It's impossible to dig a hole to China." One of the brothers with a big smile held up a jar filled with dirty coins and fancy stones and a few colorful bugs. "Maybe it is impossible to dig a hole to China, but look what we have discovered along the way."

What's hoped for may never come to pass, what's hoped for may never be realized but there's time along the way. It can be spent being hopeful or not being hopeful. It can be spent as Patsy spent her days or it can be spent in the misery of despair. Being hopeful beats its alternative in that many good things may well come to be discovered along the way.

The fourth reason why we should be hopeful, the fourth reason why we should never give up hope is that darkness cannot extinguish light. There's something we can all do that brings home that point. Find two rooms, one being in darkness and the other being in light with a door between them. Open the door and you'll find the dark room getting lighter while the light room isn't the least bit dimmed. And what's true when it comes to those twinned rooms is true as well when it comes to things spiritual.

One of the most dreadful days in 1914 when war was ravaging all of Europe, Viscount Grey, the great English statesman, sought composure by listening to a Mr. Campbell McGinnes sing the songs of the great composer Handel. Afterwards, Grey wrote a note to McGinnis in these words: "Europe it is in the most terrible trouble it's ever known in civilized times and no one can say what will be left in the end. One thing, however, is for sure, Handel's music will survive."

Grey touched on a reality when it came to things of beauty, when it came to things of light. They are eternal, indestructible, undebasable and always spiritually satisfying. That is not true of ugly things. That's not true of things of darkness.

And think, if you will, of such patrons of light as Gandhi and Mother Teresa and Abraham Lincoln and Dorothy Day. Their lives will forever be celebrated and admired; their lives will forever be a source of inspiration. That won't be true when it comes to the Hitler's and the Stalin's and the Osama Bin Ladens and the other patrons of darkness that have walked the earth. Try as it may, darkness cannot extinguish light. What may dash our hopes will not prevail.

The fifth reason why we should be hopeful, the fifth reason why we should never give up hope is that those in the know don't always know. The experts are not always right.

"There's no likelihood man can ever tap the power of the atom!" so said Robert Milliken, the Nobel Prize winner in physics in 1920. "I think there is a world market for about five computers!" so said Thomas Watson, chairman of IBM in 1943. When Alexander Graham Bell offered the head of Western Union the exclusive rights to his talking machine, president William Orton turned down the offer claiming no one could possibly be interested in an electric toy.

History is filled with countless examples of people in the know greatly miscalculating human potential. History is filled with so-called experts nowhere near accurate in their predictions of what would or would not come to pass. Crushers of hope are not always right.

The sixth and final reason why we should be hopeful, why we should never give up hope is that God is with us always. After sixteen years of service as a missionary in the heat of Africa, David Livingston returned to his native land of Scotland. During his furlough, he was asked to speak to the students of Glasgow University. His body was weakened and emaciated from his experience. Over the sixteen years in Africa, he suffered and survived twenty seven bouts of tropical fever. One of his arms hung motionless at his side, the result of it being mangled by a lion. As he stood before those students at the university, he told them what sustained him amidst the toil, the hardship, the suffering, and the loneliness. "What sustained me," he told those students, "what sustained me was Christ's promise: 'Lo, I'll be with you always!'"

What sustained Livingston through his misery is what can sustain us in our hopefulness. No matter what may come of what it is we're hoping for, we know we are not wasting our time because we know God is with us and God being with us assures a happy ending.

I'm reminded of something from the old days of Hollywood. Deborah Kerr, a leading lady in those days, was starring in the film Quo Vadis. She was being interviewed by a reporter who asked her how she was able to handle one particular scene where the lions came charging at her. In particular, he asked her if she were afraid and she said "No!" She told the reporter that she was one of those rare actresses who read the entire script of the movie before she'd assume her role. "That being the case," she said, "when those lions charged at me, I knew that Robert Taylor would come to my rescue."

We know from the script called the Gospels that even if what we're hoping for never comes to pass in this life, it will come to pass in the next. Having read that script, we needn't ever despair for a happy ending is assured us. God will rescue our hopes from the lions trying to consume them.

As far as that question "Is there hope?" goes, yes there is hope. There's hope because we'd been through bad times before and did well. There is hope because light always prevails over darkness. There's hope because "Hey, you never know!" There's hope because the experts aren't always right. There is hope because God is with us and he's given us the script and the script tells us that no matter what, things in the end will be alright.

My friends, the Advent season is a call for all of us to be hopeful. Be hopeful! Don't give up hope! Even though the bad times seem insurmountable, don't give up hope. The alternative is no way to live.

Remember Not the Things of The Past

Isaiah 43: 16-21

"...Remember not the events of the past..."

It's often best not to remember.

Three sisters shared an apartment. They were all up in years, the youngest having recently celebrated her 92nd birthday. One night, the eldest sister drew a bath. She put one foot in and paused because she couldn't remember if she was getting into the tub or was getting out of the tub. She yelled down to the middle sister to come up the stairs to help her remember. The middle sister begins to ascend the stairs and then she pauses and says: "Was I going up the stairs or was I going down the stairs?" Well, the youngest sister, taking all this in, says to herself: "I sure hope I never get that forgetful!" And she knocks on wood for good measure. She then yells to her siblings: "I'll be right there to help but there's a knock at the door I need to answer."

We can laugh at that comical exchange, but the truth is that forgetfulness is not a laughing matter. Many a family is mired in grief because Alzheimer's disease has been slowly destroying the memory of their loved one. That being said, there are times when forgetfulness can be a positive, when not remembering can be a virtue, when it's best that things from the past get expunged from our memories.

I like that story of the two men who got to talking one day. The first one said: "You know, I have a friend who has a terrible memory. The worst memory one could ever have." The second man said: "Forgets everything, huh?" And the first man replied: "No! He remembers everything."

Life Injections IV

It's that terrible sort of memory that I'd like to talk with you about today. It's the positive nature of forgetfulness I'd like to discuss with you today. Many are the times when there is something that ought not to be remembered and many are the times when there are things we need to forget.

Some of you might recall the name Donnie Moore, a pitcher for the California Angels baseball team. In early October of 1986, the Angels were nearing victory over the Boston Red Sox in the American League Championship Series. It was the ninth inning of the fifth game where they led by a score of 5 to 3. An Angel victory would clinch the American League championship and they would then move on to the World Series. The Red Sox narrowed the lead to 5 to 4 and the Angels brought in their ace relief pitcher Donnie Moore to face Red Sox hitter Dave Henderson. Moore threw two quick strikes and Henderson feebly fouled off the next pitch obviously being overpowered by Moore's speed. Instead of coming at him again with a fastball, Moore decides to throw a changeup and Henderson hits into the upper deck of the right field stands giving Boston the lead and the victory.

The Angel's players and their fans looked on in disbelief. The Angels failed to recover from that loss and Boston progressed to the World Series. Although Donnie Moore had had a terrific season, Henderson's homerun haunted him. He couldn't shake its memory. He could not forget it. Despite encouragement from his teammates, the management of the Angels as well as his family, despite their efforts to free Moore of that haunted memory, it failed to work. Moore would soon fall into deep depression. On July 19, 1989, Donnie Moore took his life.

An extreme case, for sure, but its evidence of why it can be important to forget, why remembering everything can be a terrible sort of memory. More times than one would like to think, a remembrance can attain a toxic nature, a remembrance can put a hold on happiness. It can fracture inner peace. It can debilitate tranquility. And if no effort is made to extract it from one's memory, there can be lethal repercussions.

And besides lethal repercussions, the failure to forget, remembering everything, can, at times, have tragic repercussions. Well known pastor and author Fred Buechner writes sadly of his mother who died a very lonely death as an old woman. She had been a gorgeous brunette who delighted in her physical beauty but when she lost her beauty, once her aging years took away some of her lovely features, she became, in Buechner's words, she became like a millionaire who runs out of money. With her looks gone, she felt she had nothing left to offer the world. Not unlike Greta Garbo and Marlene Dietrich, she holed herself up in her apartment never venturing outside except in disguise. In all essence, Beuchner's mother retired to the past. She retreated from the present. She missed the future.

Whether it's turning 21 or 40 or 65, whether it's an enfeebling illness, a crummy job or forced retirement, whether it's family problems or alcoholism or confinement to a nursing home, whatever might be perceived as a horrid development or a horrid situation, the temptation is great to follow Buechner's mother's lead, to disengage from the present and the future and to make the past one's home.

Some of you might recall that old film entitled *Come Back, Little Sheba*. Burt Lancaster played the male lead and Shirley Booth played the wife. Throughout the film, the Booth character kept recalling the good old days: "Remember when?" was her constant mantra. Time and again, she'd walk out onto the porch calling for little Sheba, their dog who had disappeared long ago, the dog who became the symbol for the bygone days when hopes were high and joy was plentiful. The Lancaster and Booth characters, for all intents and purposes, made the past their home. They were living what Henry David Thoreau called "lives of quiet desperation."

One of the problems with our failure to forget and our remembering everything is that it puts the past at a higher premium than the future or the present. And so when hard times come, when a dreaded change occurs in how we are living our life, it's back to yesterday we go. It's living a life of quiet desperation that we pursue. And not unlike Buechner's mother, it makes for a tragic conclusion to what may once have been a promising life.

And besides lethal and tragic consequences, the failure to forget, remembering everything, has strained and destroyed many a family and many a relationship. You might recall my telling you about a film that was once featured at a Chicago Film Festival some years ago. The plot involved a love affair between a sensitive young girl and an egocentric boy. The strength of the film lay in its portrayal of their developing relationship. It was warm and innocent and full of promise. As it happened, the boy had to leave for a year of study. Upon his return, he learns that while gone, his girlfriend had an affair. He resumes the relationship but the affair unsettles him and he can't shake it from his memory. Any chance he gets, he tells his lover he forgives her for her indiscretion while the repetition and the tone makes it obvious that he doesn't forgive her at all.

The final scene was powerful as he yelled from the couch for what may have been the 50th time: "Honey, I forgive you!" And then you hear the kitchen door slam and she walks out of his life forever.

The failure to forget has destroyed more than a few relationships. The unwillingness to not remember everything puts a tremendous strain on families where blunders and arguments and disastrous mistakes and ill chosen words can abound. The film captures well the destructive nature of holding before a friend a memory that needs to be forgotten.

I always liked that story attributed to Claire Booth founder of the Red Cross. One time a friend recalled to her a cruel thing that had happened to her some years earlier but Claire seemed not to remember the incident. "Don't you remember the wrong that was done to you?" said the friend. And Claire responded: "I distinctly remember forgetting it." If we hope to hold a family together, if we hope to keep a relationship intact, we can't be remembering everything. There are things we most definitely must remember to forget.

And then there's the matter of sin. Bruce Larson tells the story of a Catholic priest living in the Philippines, a much loved man of God who once carried a secret burden of a long ago sin buried deep in his heart. He had committed the sin many years ago during his time in the seminary. No one else knew of that sin. He repented of it, but had no peace, no inner joy, and no sense of God's forgiveness.

There was a woman in that priest's parish who deeply loved God and claimed to have a vision where she spoke with Christ and him with her. The priest, however, was skeptical of her claim and, to test her visions, he said "You say you actually speak directly with Christ in your visions? I want you to ask him what sin your priest committed while he was in the seminary. Only God would know."

The woman agreed and went home. When she returned to the church a few weeks later, the priest said: "Well, did Christ visit you in your dreams?" She replied: "Yes, he did." "And did you ask him what sin I committed in the seminary?" "Yes, I asked him." she replied. "And what did he say?" asks the priest. She replied: "He said I don't remember."

Contrary to what many of us believe, God chooses not to remember everything and God chooses to forget especially our sins. It is a wise old soul who once said: "What God has forgotten, it's no business of ours to remember."

Isaiah in our first reading beckons the Israelites to remember not the things of the past while St. Paul in our second reading says that he's given no thought to what lies behind but pushes to what lies ahead. You could say that they are railing against that terrible sort of memory that remembers everything and hailing the sort of memory that forgets what needs to not be remembered.

So, it behooves us to be a bit more forgetful. It could well keep a home run, a mistake, from taking on lethal repercussions. It could well keep the past from imprisoning us from the future. It could well keep a relationship from destruction and some past sin from getting the upper hand it doesn't deserve. My friends! Heed the words of Isaiah. When bad things happen, remember not the things of the past, the things of long ago remember not.

Being a Somebody

Mark 9:30-37

"...they had been arguing as to who was the most important..."

What happens to provide worth and value.

The clerk in a posh hotel greeted a black gentleman who asked if a room were available. The fellow didn't appear very distinguished and so the clerk responded in the negative. By happenstance, the hotel manager came by and recognizes the black gentleman as Hank Aaron of the Atlanta Braves whose face was on the cover of every sports page for having broken Babe Ruth's record for career home runs. He whispers to the clerk that bit of information and the now red faced clerk immediately calls out to Aaron and apologetically informs him that a room was indeed available and it would be ready in a few short minutes. After a brief pause, he says to the famous ballplayer: "Mr. Aaron, why didn't you tell me you're a somebody?" Hank Aaron retorted: "Son, everybody is a somebody!"

I agree with Hank Aaron, everybody is a somebody, but I also happen to believe that there are different grades of somebody and that some people are more of a somebody than are others. And in my humble opinion, it has little to do with the marks and measures which society normally tends to use to establish those grades and to make that distinction.

First of all, I do not believe that being a somebody has anything to do with wealth. There was a play that both delighted and discomforted British audiences in the early part of the century. It was J. M. Barrie's satire: *Admiral Crichton*. In the play, a pompous English millionaire and his equally pompous daughters are shipwrecked on an island along with all of the servants whom they brought along to serve them, one of whom was a butler named

Crichton. It would be Crichton's skill and resourcefulness that made survival possible. He creates electric lights and piped water and many other instruments necessary to keep them all alive and well. Eventually, Crichton emerges as the natural Lord of the island and, in a reversal of roles, that pompous millionaire and his pompous daughters begin serving him.

The point J. M. Barrie tried to make with his play was that once removed from wealth and all of its trappings, a person's true worth and stature emerges. In essence, "wealth does not make the man."

Now, it might be that you're a somebody in the eyes of a Wall Street executive but to be a real somebody comes down to something other than a bank account. It comes down to what you might do and give for the sake of the health and well being of another. It rests upon the qualities you exhibit apart from the wealth you may have happened to accumulate. What made Crichton a somebody was his unselfishness, his resourcefulness, and most especially his willingness to exercise those qualities for the benefit of someone else.

And right beside wealth sits clothes. What you happen to be wearing does not make you a somebody. A number of years ago there died in Paris a woman who had the dubious distinction of being the best dressed woman in Europe. After her death, it was found that the chief item of her legacy to the world was a wardrobe consisting of a thousand sets of clothes which meant a thousand dresses, a thousand hats and a thousand pairs of shoes. At about the same time, there died in London a man who had one suit of clothes. It was a blue suit with a red color. Of the two individuals, the man and not the woman proved to be a somebody. The man's name was William Booth, the founder of the Salvation Army.

You might be a somebody in the eyes of the fashion world. You might be a somebody in the eyes of Ralph Lauren or Tommy Hilfiger. But to be a real somebody comes down to something more than clothes. It rests not upon what you happen to be wearing, but upon what you are doing or how you are behaving within the set of clothes you happen to have on.

And right beside wealth and clothes, there is brain power. Your IQ is not what makes you a somebody. Some months back, I was called to the special care nursery of Sisters Hospital to baptize a baby who was about to die. The baby was born with a birth defect known as anencephaly, a defect involving the brain stem. Quite literally, the baby was born without any cerebral function and without cerebral function it would be only a matter of time before death would claim that life. I baptized the baby and comforted the parents and I, as well as the nursing staff, fully expected that baby to die within minutes if not hours. The minutes and hours fell into days and the baby was sent home with the parents under hospice care.

I would discover shortly thereafter that I had performed the marriage of that baby's grandparents and so we were reunited and had a talk. I counseled them to love their grandchild as much as possible but also relayed to them the sad news that a child in his condition may live for three months at best but not much longer. The baby whose name was Paiten J. Meyers-Brogan lived a total of eighteen months. I was called to the house and to Children's Hospital several times along the way with the expectation that death was near, but somehow little Paiten survived those emergencies. What I witnessed throughout that time was how big an impact Paiten was having on his family as well as those to whom they were close to and near. His funeral took place at Our Lady of Victory Basilica before hundreds of people. If you want to talk about a somebody, Paiten was it. This child born with no brain power at all touched more hearts and influenced more individuals and made a bigger difference in people's lives than many whose brain power is off the charts, than many whose IQ would rank them among the smartest and the brightest in the world.

You might be a somebody as far as Harvard University or MIT is concerned, but to be a real somebody comes down to something more than how smart you happen to be or where you ranked on your SAT scores. It comes down to how you affect people, how much love you happen to generate. It comes down to how much of a positive difference you make in the lives of those you happen to be near.

And besides wealth and clothes and brainpower, there is also the matter of fame. How famous you are does not make you a somebody. Some years ago, I read an article about Henry Nouwen, a catholic monk and renowned writer. It told of how Nouwen had become so overwhelmed by a busy speaking and writing career that he took up residence in a monastery that cared for severely handicapped individuals. He did so to maintain his spiritual center.

The writer of the article went to that monastery for the interview and, when he arrived, asked the receptionist as to where he might find the famous monk. She told him to go down the hallway to the third floor and he would be in the second room on the left. The reporter fully expected the room to be an office filled with books and he believed he'd find Nouwen there gently ministering to the needs of some afflicted soul. When he got to the third floor and pushed open the door of the second room on his left, he found himself in a public bathroom. Believing he had misunderstood the directions, he asked the janitor who was scrubbing the toilets as to how he might find Henry Nouwen. The man looked up and said: "You found him! I'm Henry Nouwen!"

You might be a somebody as far as the Enquirer magazine and TV's *Inside Edition* is concerned, but to be a real somebody comes down to more than fame and notoriety. It comes down to humility. It comes down to not 'Lording' it over others. It comes down to a willingness to get your hands dirty, to clean toilets and messes if necessary. It comes down to a willingness to perform those menial tasks usually considered beneath someone of celebrity status. Henry Nouwen had the fame. He was a celebrity. But what made him a somebody was his humility.

Besides wealth and clothes and brainpower and fame not making you a somebody, so it goes as well with your pedigree. The family into which you were born does not a somebody make. I recall here two boys who shared a similar birth date. One was African American and the other a Caucasian of Polish descent. The latter grew up outside of Chicago to a very well to do family while the former grew up in a ghetto in Daytona Beach, Florida to a family who abandoned him. What's interesting is what came of the two boys. The African American child is now 27 years of age and his name is Roland Fryer. He's a Harvard graduate and he teaches economics and he's been working hard to help kids who, like himself, came from a difficult background. The Caucasian child of

Polish descent went to Harvard as well. He's serving time in a federal prison. His name is Ted Kaczynski, the Unabomber.

You might be a somebody because you have a famous last name or because you were born with a silver spoon in your mouth. But to be a real somebody comes down to more than a pedigree. It comes down to what you do with the pedigree. It comes down to what you make of your background no matter how privileged or pitiful it happens to be.

And then there's the matter of your physical condition. Neither your muscles nor your beauty makes you a somebody. There is a Zen Buddhist story of a wealthy man who always desired the approval of a certain Zen Master. He purchased an expensive tea set overlaid with the most exquisite of jewels. He invited that certain Zen Master to tea. At last, he thought, I will impress the holy man beyond all question. But when the Zen Master came to tea, he said nothing about the tea set. After he left, the man was so angry that he smashed the set into a million pieces. The servant swept up the fragments, took them home and painstakingly glued the pieces together. Even though the tea set was no where near as beautiful as it once had been, the servant was sufficiently proud of it to invite that same Zen Master to have tea with him. When the Zen Master saw the repaired tea set with its cracks and its glue, he could not stop talking about its beauty. The moral of the story is that it's often the nicks and dents and scratches that makes something beautiful.

What's true for making something beautiful is also true for making someone a somebody. I'm reminded of the story of the man who died and went to heaven. He stood before God and God asked him: "Where are your wounds?" The man replied: "I have none!" God looked at him with a scowl and said: "You mean to tell me that in the course of your lifetime you found nothing worth fighting for?"

You might be a somebody in the eyes of some bodybuilding magazine or in the eyes of some judges at a beauty pageant, but to be a real somebody, to be a real beauty, involves finding something worth fighting for and then being willing to sustain the wounds it might take to further along the worthwhile venture. It involves a willingness to get nicked so justice could be served, the willingness to get scratched and dented in service to humanity. It involves a willingness to take on the scars necessary to make something beautiful for God.

And then, finally, there is the matter of your rank. Being a General or a President or a CEO does not a somebody make. I believe Tom Brokaw captured that truth in his book *The Greatest Generation*[12]. The book is a memoir of the recollections of men and women who fought in the Second World War. Torn from the security of home, they were sent off to fight in Europe and in the Pacific. They lived in the mud and the cold. Many died. Many were wounded. Yet hardly a one complained or ever looked for pity. The overwhelming majority were plain soldiers, sailors, pilots, or nurses, ordinary men and women just doing their job. Those members of the "greatest generation" are all somebody's not because of the rank they held but because in their own small way they made a sacrifice, they made a contribution to the world. Without them, we wouldn't enjoy the freedoms we have today.

The disciples in our Gospel were talking amongst themselves as to who was the greatest. And I'm sure that they used the same criteria society happened to apply. The greatest in their eyes had to do with wealth and clothes and brainpower and pedigree and beauty and rank. Jesus set them straight. He said that if you want to be great, if you want to be a somebody, you need to be a servant. You need to put yourself last not first. And when he picked up that little child, he got into wounds and sacrifice and unselfishness and touching life in a significant way because that's what usually follows the acceptance of a child into your life.

So if you want to be a somebody, forget the fancy clothes; forget being a millionaire; forget having credentials before and after your name; forget the plastic surgery and the steroids; forget moving to a better neighborhood. Do what Jesus said and you'll be a somebody in the eyes of God. That sure beats being a somebody in the eyes of Wall Street or Inside Edition or Harvard University or whatever it is society might happen to use to make that distinction.

The 24/7 Mentality

Mark 6: 30-34

"...Come by yourselves to an out of the way place and rest a while..."

Sleep deprivation sits at the heart of many a malady.

There was once a billboard for a hospital's emergency room. In the background was a picture of planets orbiting in space and in the foreground the words: "And on the seventh day, God rested. We don't!" It was a clever advertisement for the 24 hour service of that hospital's emergency room yet, at the same time, it crystallized a growing problem sweeping across our country and that's the problem of a 24/7 mentality. In contrast to God, we believe in a seven day work week. We're of the opinion that rest is for the faint of heart. Time off is for the lazy. The Sabbath is for the weak.

The Surgeon General recently reported that one in four American adults claim no leisure time activities. A Bureau of Labor statistic reads that average married couples work 26% longer each year than couples did thirty years ago. A University of Michigan study found that free time among children ages 12 and under declined from 40% in 1981 to 25% in 1997. As those studies and reports appear to indicate, more than a few of us have bought into the 24/7 mentality. More than a few of us have it in our heads that rest and relaxation and leisure are anathema, that life is all about work and labor and burning the midnight oil. As a result, problems have most definitely ensued.

Joe DeLamielleure, the Hall of Fame guard of the Buffalo Bills, is a regular on WGR talk radio. He has said many times during this past football season that he believes that it's a lack of rest and relaxation that's behind many of the coaching errors that occur during a football game, that the 7AM to midnight, 7 days a week work schedule of NFL coaches has resulted in their minds never getting proper rest. That, in fact, sleep deprivation is behind many of the bungled decisions which even the most seasoned of coaches now have a habit of making

One of the best books I've read this year is *Outliers* [13] by Malcolm Gladwell and in one of the chapters of that book he talks of airplane crashes and amongst the many reasons he cites for their sad reality, sleep deprivation sits near the top.

There has been evidence that the Challenger, Chernobyl and Three Mile Island disasters were all caused in part by decisions made by people in critical positions who were sleep deprived.

There's a Dr. Forest Tennant, one of America's foremost experts on drug addiction, who has tied that growing malady to sleep deprivation. According to Tennant, sleep is the only time the brain has available for the reproduction of certain chemicals that are critical to keeping the mind and body balanced and in good health. If those chemicals are not produced and released during sleep, symptoms will develop and occur causing the sufferer to seek relief through drugs, in some cases legal and in other cases not.

And besides drug addiction, bad decision making, poor performances and airplane crashes having a link with sleep deprivation, so can a case be made for poor grades being a result of a lack of sleep.

Statistics have found that most teenagers need a little more than nine hours of sleep every night that it's during slumber time that many of their hormones get released which, if not released, results in their inability to function to the best of their ability. It's no accident that teens do the poorest in courses taught in the early morning hours of a school day. And studies have also shown that students who don't get enough sleep achieve far lower grades than students who are well rested.

So, needless to say, the 24/7 mentality with its demonizing of rest and relaxation and leisure has not come without its price. Sleep deprivation and fatigue has taken its toll on the performance levels, the decision making ability, and the overall functioning of countless numbers of people. It can well be said that God got it right and we got it wrong. Outworking God is not a good idea.

And it's not a good idea not just because of the negatives I've just referenced, but it's not a good idea because of all the positives that rest and relaxation and leisure have been known to deliver.

Aging composer Johannes Brahms is said to have shocked his friends and colleagues with the announcement that he would no longer write music. "Why shouldn't I enjoy my old age?" he explained to those saddened by his news. "I'll not write another note!" And so it was, Brahms retired and seemed comfortable with his new freedom. Yet, several months later, he debuts a new composition. "I thought you weren't going to write any more music!" said a friend. "I wasn't." he said, "but after a few days of leisure, I was so happy at the thought of not writing, that music came to me naturally, music came to me without effort.

When breathers have been taken, when rest gets provided, there's often a clearing of the mind that helps to make room for new ideas, new thoughts, and innovative thinking.

Novelist Herman Wouk remembers the stressful days preparing his *Caine Mutiny Court Martial* for its opening night on Broadway. When scenes were being re-written and everyone was tense and harried, Wouk went to the director on Friday afternoon and told him he was leaving to observe the Sabbath and would not be back till Saturday night. "You can't do that!" screamed the director, "This is the most critical period for a project in which people have invested hundreds of thousands of dollars!" Undaunted, Wouk left to observe the Sabbath. When Wouk returned the following night, he was mentally refreshed and, as a result, was able to see problems in a new light. The re-writes were easier and changes got made that improved the quality of the play. On opening night, the *Caine Mutiny Court Martial* was performed in flawless fashion.

In 1940, when Great Britain's very survival was in question, when their only hope appeared to be help from the United States, the then President Franklin Roosevelt decided to take a two week Caribbean vacation aboard the US Tuscaloosa. You can imagine the barrage of criticism that followed that decision, criticism from both sides of the Atlantic. That decision, that time away, that period of rest and relaxation helped Roosevelt to think more clearly, to think beyond traditional politics. Home from his time away, FDR concocted a daring new idea, the Lend-Lease Plan.

That policy, that plan provided ships and supplies to Great Britain and those ships and supplies helped that beleaguered country survive the grueling winter of 1940.

One of the positives to be had from rest and relaxation and leisure is that it serves as a breeding ground for creativity. It serves up new thoughts and new ideas held at bay by tiredness, kept out of sight because our eyes were too heavy to see them.

And besides serving up new thoughts and new ideas; rest and leisure and relaxation also helps us to keep things in perspective. It awakens us to priorities missed in a 24/7 environment.

The late comedian Eddie Cantor lived in just such an environment. He pursued his career on stages across the country. His grandmother would often say to him: "Don't hurry so much and run around so much or you'll miss the scenery!" He never paid attention to what she said until one night the curtain came down after one of his performances. He was basking in the glory and the excitement his performance had provided him when he received a telegram from his wife. The telegram announced that his fourth daughter had just been born. It was then that his grandmother's words echoed in his ears. Eddie Cantor, from that time forward, made it a point to regularly take time off so he wouldn't miss the scenery.

The 24/7 mentality, so prevalent today, allows no time for scenery, no time to stop and take notice of what happens to be going on around us. And that means missed opportunities to recognize blessings and moments that we might never see again, blessings and moments which one day we may terribly regret our not having taken the time to notice.

A group of children were once given the task of saying things about God and one of them wrote: God gives us a lot of days so we would not try and do everything at once. What a wonderful insight as to God's call to slow down and enjoy life one day at a time.

I always liked the story of a successful business man who visited an Indian village. As he walked along, he saw a man under a tree doing nothing. The business man stopped and said: "Hey, Chief, don't you think it's time to be up and about doing something productive?" The man under the tree looked up and said: "Why?" The business man said: "Why? So you can get a job, earn some money and make something of yourself!" The man under the tree smiled and said: "Why?" The now exasperated business man said: "Why? So you can make money, start a savings account and someday you can retire and enjoy life!" The man under the tree answered: "I'm enjoying life, now!"

No rest, no relaxation, no leisure can not only keep us from enjoying the scenery but it can keep us from enjoying life now.

And then finally amongst the positives of rest and relaxation and leisure is the fact of its putting us in good company. Winston Churchill said once that he could do without his cigars but he could not do without his nap. Henry Ford and Albert Einstein were known for taking 20 minute cat naps each workday. And I'll never forget Edward Roberts of Lancaster Seminary. He heard his pastor make the announcement that he was not going to take a summer vacation because the devil never does. That prompted Roberts to go home and read the Gospels whereupon he found that in his three years of active ministry there was mentioned ten periods of time when Jesus took a rest and that wasn't counting the Sabbath. Roberts then figured he's rather follow the lead of Jesus instead of the devil's lead.

And consider if you will the book of Genesis. Note in that book that God doesn't bless the day when he made the beasts of the earth, the birds of the sky and the fish of the sea. He didn't even bless the day when he made us male and female. Genesis reads that God blessed the seventh day and hallowed it. You could say that God only blessed the day on which he did nothing. Rest and relaxation and leisure indeed puts us in good company and besides it's blessed by God.

In today's Gospel, Jesus is advocating for his disciples to rest a while and you might say he's advocating for us to do the same. You could well say that he's siding with God when it comes to the six day vs. seven day work week.

My friends, resist the 24/7 mentality. Don't get yourself sleep deprived. Make it a point to occasionally go away and rest a while. Do so and you and your family will be the better for it. You'll think more clearly. You'll not miss the scenery. You'll be more creative. You'll be in good company. You'll be blessed by God.

Loneliness

John 14: 15-21

"...I will not leave you orphaned..."

There are many a reason as to why we may be lonely.

I heard of a fellow named Herman who was a television repair man back in the 1950s. One day he was dispatched to service the television of an old man named Jake who lived alone. When Herman inspected Jakes' television, he found that it was missing a tube. Herman replaced it in a matter of minutes and spent the next 20 minutes chatting amiably with Jake, and then he left for his next call. A week later, Jake reported that his television was on the blink again and Herman went to fix it. This time, he discovered that a different tube was missing. He replaced that tube and once more had a pleasant conversation with Jake. The following week, Jake called the repair shop and once again complained that his TV was on the blink. When Herman opened the back of the television, he found a different tube was missing and it was then that he came to realize that Jake had been purposely removing the tubes, doing so because he was lonely and having Herman come over provided him with the company he longed to have.

I'm reminded of the made for TV movie *Door to Door* which was the true to life story of Billy Porter, a salesman who suffered from cerebral palsy. William H Macy won an Emmy playing the lead role. Porter's best customer (a part played by Kathy Baker) proved to be a woman who never failed to purchase a multitude of items and so he frequently came to her home. When that customer died, her family had Billy come over one last time and they showed him the rooms he had never seen. The rooms were stacked from top to bottom with unopened boxes of all the things he sold her. What Herman was for Jake, Billy Porter was for his best customer and that was a respite from her loneliness, the company she longed to have.

There are plenty of Jake's and plenty of that Kathy Baker character in the world in which we live. Loneliness for all intents and purposes has reached epic proportions. Psychologist Paul Tournier called loneliness the most devastating malady of our time. Billy Graham declared it the problem that bothers more people than any other problem. According to Los Angeles author and psychiatrist Dr. Leonard Zunin, humanity's biggest problem is loneliness. And the sad truth is that more people suffer from it today than have ever suffered from it before. And that is true for many reasons. First of all our demographics have changed.

According to the most recent census, one quarter of our nation's households, 27.3 million of them, consists of just one person. In 1950, less than 10% of all households made that claim.

Someone from my old neighborhood of Black Rock was interviewed in regards to the recent closing of churches. She made an interesting point about why the diocese had to downsize in the way that they did. She told how she lived in a house at the corner of Amherst and Howell on the short side of Howell. There were four houses on her side of the street and four houses on the other. She said when she was growing up, 10 people lived in her house. "Now," she said, "there aren't 10 people living on my entire block."

I am 61 years of age and I go back to the day of extended families living under one roof. My grandparents my aunt and my uncle, my mom and dad, my brother and I, we all lived in the same house. And we were the norm and not the exception.

That, of course, has all changed. The extended family scene is no longer. As the statistics have shown, you're more likely to find an empty house than a full one. You're more likely to find people living alone than find them living with others. Aloneness does not necessarily translate into loneliness but it does substantially increase its chance of rearing its ugly head.

And then, there's the reality of the mobility embedded into the culture of today's society, that too has been a cause for the increase in loneliness. I hate to keep harking back to the old days but back

Life Injections IV

in the day, once you got a job you stayed in that job till you died or retired. My grandfather worked at American Radiator for 41 years, my uncle Steve for 45 years and my Uncle Chester for 50 years. Most of the factories of old held onto the same workforce for a long time.

Today you find very few factories, you find companies constantly changing ownership. You're lucky if you can hold onto a job for more than five years. People today are constantly changing jobs and many of those jobs land them in another city. It's not unusual for parents today to have their children scattered across the country. Be it child or be it parent, the increasing mobility embedded in the culture of today can find either one living far apart from the other and the aloneness that breeds can substantially increase the chance of feeling lonely.

And then, as a cause for loneliness, there's the demise of the social groups and the social activities that once eased its pain. Look at scouting, woman's clubs, moose lodges, and Kiwanis's clubs, they all show diminishing numbers. PTA membership has dropped from 12 million in 1984 to 6 million today. Membership in the Jaycees is down 44%. My brother has taken up bowling in his old age and now bowls in a mixed couple's league and he tells me that in Northern Pittsburgh, which is an area that would encompass Cheektowaga and Amherst and Lancaster combined, there are but 2 bowling alleys with only 12 lanes in each. Participation in bowling leagues has decreased 45%.

And besides these huge drop offs in sports leagues and social groups, statistics also show that entertaining friends and acquaintances in one's family home has diminished substantially. Dinner parties are held far less often than they once had been. And what all this means is that fewer are the opportunities for human contact that once helped to dispel the feelings of loneliness.

And then you have as a feeder of loneliness all these new technologies which at one level has increased human interaction and yet on another level has decreased that interaction.

There is an interesting anecdote involving the inventor of the transistor radio. He was driving to a conference where he was to be honored for his new innovation in radio service. He stopped for a bite to eat and sitting across from him was a family and he noticed his invention, the transistor radio, sitting in front of the teenage children with a line running from the radio into their ear. They were so engrossed in what they were listening to on the radio that there was absolutely no conversation going on between them and their parents. The man left the restaurant wondering if humankind might have been better served without his invention.

What the inventor witnessed with his transistor radio is common fare today with the radio being replaced by the I Phone. It's not unusual to find family members engrossed in talking or text messaging during the course of a meal with a face-to-face conversation failing to occur at all. Technology has helped communication in one way but it has destroyed communication in another. Text messaging and Facebook and e-mail and internet chat rooms have fostered many a relationship but has served as well to put many at a distance from those physically in their presence, those who in the past had counted on them for conversation. Now that someone sits there lost in cyberspace, absorbed by a hand held device that has their rapt attention. It can be said in many circles that technology has fostered loneliness.

And besides technology fostering loneliness, affluence has done the same. Back in the day when our grandparents and great grandparents first came to this country, survival was pretty much the only item on the docket. They had to cope with the Great Depression, they had to learn a new language, they had to find a job, and they needed to save for a home. They struggled valiantly to survive the harsh dictates and harsh realities of that time in history and that managed to consume all of their time and energy and every ounce of their creativity. You could say that they neither had the time nor the zest to be lonely.

That is most certainly not the case with us. We, their offspring, are the beneficiaries of the affluence and the privileges that they'd worked so hard to provide. We no longer have to spend huge chunks of time and energy and creativity on many of the issues that absorbed their time and their attention. Survival is no longer the only item on our dockets thus leaving us with plenty of time and a great deal of energy to probe beneath the surface of our lives often unearthing a profound sense of loneliness.

Life Injections IV

Then you have the higher things in life that can also be a source of loneliness. Things like saying no when everyone else is saying yes, taking a stand with no supporting cast, rallying behind a cause no one is willing to support.

Then, there's the fastest growing problem of our time and that's diminished hearing. More and more people are afflicted with a hearing impairment leaving them unable to participate in conversations, unable to hear well enough to understand what it is someone may be trying to say. That sense of isolation breeds yet another source of loneliness.

When all is said and done, there are many reasons, many factors, and many causes for loneliness being the malady that it is, for loneliness growing in epic proportions. So the Gospel we heard read is a timely one, a needed one for the growing number caught in the throes of loneliness. That's because Jesus is telling his disciples and in turn telling us that he will not leave us orphans, that he'll never abandon us, will never leave us feeling alone.

Robert Byrd, back in 1974, spent five months in a hut buried beneath the ice caps of the Rose Basin deep into Antarctica. He was the only living creature south of latitude 72. Blizzards roared across his hut. The cold plunged to 82° below zero. He was completely surrounded by unending night. One day, he finds to his horror that he was being slowly poisoned by the carbon monoxide escaping from his stove. He did what he could to fix the problem but to no avail. Help was 123 miles away and could not possibly reach him any time soon. Believing that death was near, he took out a sheet of paper and began to write a philosophy of life. The first words he wrote were: "I am not alone!" There was in him a tremendous sense of the presence of God. He felt God was with him and that sustained him till help arrived, sustained him from succumbing to the power and the pain of loneliness.

The story is reminiscent of Corrie Ten Boom, a prisoner in one of Hitler's death camps. She wrote that what got her through her loneliness, what got her through her terrible ordeal was a sense that there was no pit so deep that God was not deeper still.

Put that together with the loneliness Jesus felt upon the cross, the loneliness the apostles felt upon Christ's death. Put that together with the loneliness Lincoln felt in the midst of the Civil War, the loneliness Martin Luther King Junior felt in that Birmingham jail and the loneliness Nelson Mandela endured in his 27 year imprisonment and you have not only the sense that God is with us in our loneliness, but that the loneliness puts us in tremendous company.

My friends, may that truth and that reality help ease the weight of the loneliness you may be feeling. And if you're one of the fortunate few not burdened by loneliness, be what Herman was to Jake. Be what Billy Porter was to his best customer. Be the company some lonely soul longs to have

Saying Nice Things

Matthew 3: 13-17

"...This is my beloved son in whom I am well pleased..."

Blessed are the recipients of affirmation.

I recently came across the story of an elderly couple who were celebrating their 50th wedding anniversary. The husband was asked what the secret was to a successful marriage and he proceeded to tell of how as a young man he worked so hard that he didn't have time to date, but then, he said, "I met Sarah and she swept me off my feet! It wasn't long thereafter that we decided to get married. On the day of the wedding," so he continued, "my wife's father took me aside and handed me a small gift and then proceeded to tell me that within that gift was all I needed to know to have a happy marriage. Well, as you might imagine," said the elderly husband, "I fumbled with the paper and the ribbon. When I finally got the box open, I came upon a gold watch. I picked it up and opened it and there across the face of the watch Sarah's dad had sketched a sentence, a sentence I would see whenever I checked the time. The sentence read: 'Say something nice to Sarah!' I do that every day and that's why my marriage has lasted 50 years."

I tell that story because I'd like to talk with you today about saying nice things to people. I'd like to talk with you about affirmation. Not only is it the key to a successful marriage but it's the key to many other things in life as well. Many a life has been richly blessed thanks to an affirming word.

For eight years, a struggling writer wrote an incredible number of short stories and articles for publication and, for eight years, all he received were letters of rejection. He was about to abandon his efforts when a returned manuscripts had a note sketched across it. It read: "Nice try!" Not too many would rank that comment very high on the encouragement scale, but for this particular writer it meant the world. It brought tears to his eyes. It gave him new hope. Shortly thereafter, one of his books did get accepted for publication and that book helped him become one of the most influential writers of the 1970s. I'm speaking of Alex Haley and the book I'm referring to is *Roots*[14].

There is a similar story involving a young man who wrote a letter to his old English teacher declaring that he was heartbroken, he no longer had the desire to live. That teacher wrote back with a letter filled with praise as to the young man's ability and talent and intelligence. That praise did wonders for that young man. It propelled him to pursue a career as a writer. We're talking about H.G. Wells.

Two of literatures finest authors may never have graced us with their wares had it not been for a word of affirmation, had it not been for the fact that nice things were said to them. The key to the unveiling of a talent, the key to the emergence of a skill that may be of immense benefit to our world may well rest upon the utterance of a positive word, a written or vocal statement of praise.

And so it can be as well for a person's ability to make it through life. There's a small exhibit in the Smithsonian Institute that contains the personal effects found in Abraham Lincoln's pockets the night he was killed. On display is a small handkerchief embroidered "A. Lincoln," a pen knife, a spectacle case repaired with cotton strings, a Confederate dollar bill, and then there was a series of worn-out newspaper clippings extolling Lincoln's accomplishments as president. It was obvious that those clippings were read over and over again. Abraham Lincoln, one of the greatest men ever born, needed to be nurtured by affirmation. He needed it to get him through the difficult times when criticism came his every way, the difficult times when never was heard an encouraging word.

There is this moving story concerning Sr. Helen Mrosia who taught a third-grade class at St. Mary's School in Morris, Minnesota. One day she passed out two sheets of paper and asked the students to list the names of all the other kids in the class leaving a space or two between each name. Then she had them think of the nicest thing they could say about each of the classmates listed on those sheets of paper and then they were to write it down next to their name. She then collected the sheets, took them home and then wrote the names of each of her students on separate sheets of paper and collated under the name all the nice things that were said about them. She distributed those sheets the following day and watched all kinds of smiles appear on the faces of her students. Nothing more was said about it the rest of the year and the class moved on to the fourth grade.

About 20 years later, Sister Mrosia got word that one of her students from that third-grade class was killed in Vietnam and the parents wanted desperately for her to come to the funeral and so she did. After the funeral, the boy's parents came up to her and showed her what was in his pocket when he was killed. It was two worn-out pieces of paper that had been taped and folded and refolded many times. They were the papers she had given him 20 years earlier listing all the nice things his classmates had to say about him.

As you can see from Abraham Lincoln and that soldier in Vietnam, people crave and cherish affirmation, people long for and nurture nice things said about them. It's more vital to their well-being and psyche than the food they eat or the beverage they consume.

That part was driven home quite tragically and dramatically back in the 13th century. Frederick II ruled Sicily and he had this belief that we're all born with a common language which he suspected might be one dating back to the time of Jesus, Hebrew or perhaps Aramaic. To test this belief, he had newborn infants taken away from their natural mothers and given over to foster mothers. He instructed the foster mothers to physically care for the babies but not to speak to them. He wanted to learn what language the child would naturally speak. The experiment ended in disaster as each and every infant met with death. They could not live without the caressing and the cooing and loving words of another human being.

Affirmation has shown itself to be an element critical to life. One cannot, in essence, live without it. From birth all the way to death it is essential to a person's survival. As evidenced by what was in the pockets of Abraham Lincoln as well as that soldier killed in

Vietnam, affirming words are held onto for life. That's how precious and how revered they happen to be.

Affirming words are also at the heart of our ability to function at a maximum capacity. I read an interesting piece recently that concerns the fact that in the early days of radio when performers worked in silent studios, many of them found it impossible to perform to the best of their ability. It was all due to the fact that there was no one in the studio to applaud them, no one in the studio to affirm their work. The powers to be had bleachers brought into the radio station and whenever a performance was called for, an audience would fill its seats.

One of the first people in America ever to be paid a salary of one million dollars was Charles Schwab. He was deemed by Andrew Carnegie to be worthy of that salary because he had the uncanny knack of getting the workers under his charge to perform to the maximum of their ability. Those who worked for Schwab not only produced at a faster rate but everything they produced was of the highest quality. His factories, by a long shot, were head and shoulders above all the rest. The secret of Schwab's success rested in affirmation. Schwab was anxious to praise and loathe to find fault and that proved to make all the difference in the world when it came to workers performing to their highest levels.

I read where they recently did an analysis of workers in America and found that the number one cause of their dissatisfaction and the lack of a positive performance rested on the failure of their superiors to give them any credit. When Bob Hope was asked why he didn't retire and go fishing, his classic response was that fish don't applaud. The key to enjoying one's job, the key to functioning well, rests in affirmation and praise and kind words. Give a person applause, shower him or her with praise and observe the glow of happiness that will surround their work.

And, finally, affirmation is the key to realizing one's potential. A traveling portrait painter stopped in a small town. Looking out the window of his hotel room, he spots the town bum and decides to paint him. The bum looks dirty, he was unshaven and he wore bedraggled clothing. The painter painted him instead as a beautiful looking man in this distinguished suit. He had the town bum come to his room and he showed him the painting. "That's not me," he said. "Yes it is,' said the artist, "it's the man I see inside you, it's the man you can become." Buoyed by that positive image and those words of encouragement and praise, that man would ultimately change his life and become what that painter envisioned him to be.

Some of you might recall that very same story captured on stage in *The Man of La Mancha*. Don Quixote, the lead character, comes upon a woman named La Donza who happened to be a prostitute. Her appearance was anything but beautiful, her demeanor anything but distinguished, her attitude anything but pleasant. Don Quixote calls attention to her beauty and how special she happens to be. He calls her by the name Dulcinea which means "my lady," "my princess." The only response from La Donza was her rebuff. At the end of the play, Don Quixote is on his deathbed and who should come to see him is this distinguished and well-dressed woman pulsing with elegance. At first Quixote failed to recognize her and she tells him of the time they met and the affirmation he provided her. Looking at her, Quixote smiles and said you are Dulcinea. He would die shortly thereafter and the play ends with the former La Donza looking at the audience and proudly proclaiming, my name is Dulcinea.

So it can go with many who live on life's edge, so it can go with many a bad girl or a bad boy. The potential is there for positive transformation and many times it rests upon a word of affirmation, a word of praise, the saying of nice things.

We are celebrating today the baptism of Jesus and you'll note in the Gospel reading how the baptism concludes with God proclaiming: "You are my beloved son in whom I am well pleased!" We have here the public life of Jesus being launched by affirmation. And it could well be said that those affirming words from God gave Jesus the impetus to preach the Gospel despite all the problems and controversies and the pain and suffering that would entail.

I always liked that joke where it's asked as to why Jesus turned out so well and the answer is that it was because Mary and Joseph treated him as though he was the son of God. So my friends, treat people as though they are sons or daughters of God. Affirm those you're close to or near. Be anxious to praise and loathe to find fault.

You may help unveil a talent or a skill likened to that of an Alex Haley or an H.G. Wells. You may find your nice and kind words in the pockets of a man or woman whom you had praised many years earlier and had probably forgotten that you did. You may be the studio audience someone needed to perform well or the one the doctor ordered for a life to be redeemed. You may find your marriage lasting 50 years. My friends, be affirming, be people of praise, say nice things to people. God may well mark you as someone with whom he is well pleased.

Essentials

Ecclesiastes 1: 2; 2: 21-23

"...all things are vanity..."

What's essential for life is invisible to the eye.

My friend, the late Dr. Ernest Campbell, former pastor of The Riverside Church in New York City, once told a story of a woman who bought a parrot in a local pet store because she was lonely. She took the bird home, but after a couple of days, she returned to the store to complain because the bird hadn't as yet spoken one word. "Does it have a mirror?" the pet store owner asked. "Parrots like to look at themselves in the mirror and maybe that's why the parrot hasn't as yet spoken." So the lady bought a mirror and returned home. The next day, she was back in the store because the bird still hadn't made a sound. "What about a ladder?" the store owner asked. "Parrots enjoy walking up and down a ladder and maybe that's why the parrot hasn't as yet said a word." So she bought a ladder and returned home. She was back in the store the next day for the bird still hadn't as yet said anything." Does the parrot have a swing?" the owner asked. "Birds enjoy relaxing on a swing." So she bought a swing and went home again. The next day she returned yet one more time but this time she announced that the parrot had died. "I'm terribly sorry to hear that!" said the owner of the pet store. "Did the bird ever say anything before it died?" "Yes," answered the lady, "it said: Don't they sell any parrot food at that pet store?"

I begin with that humorous story because I'd like to talk with you today about the essentials of life, talk with you about the necessary and indispensable elements that make for a whole and fruitful life.

Back in 1900, the average person living in the United States wanted 782 different things and considered eighteen of them essential.

Today, the average person wants 500 things and considers a 100 of them essential. And if truth be told, a lot of those essentials aren't much different from the ladder, the mirror, and the swing mentioned in my opening story. And not unlike that parrot, our pursuit of those alleged essentials can leave us starving for what we really need to make life fruitful and whole.

My niece Julie, who died eleven years ago, has on her gravestone a sentence from French author Saint-Exupery's *Little Prince* [15], a sentence she often quoted. The sentence reads: "What is essential is invisible to the eye." That's especially true when it comes to life and that's especially true when it comes to what we need to make life fruitful and whole. Take the matter of hope.

Napoleon Hill tells of a successful cosmetics manufacturer who decided to retire at the age of 65. Each year thereafter, his friends and former business associates gave him a birthday party and tried to find out the secret of his special cosmetics formula. But year after year he refused to reveal his secret. "Maybe, I'll tell you next year!" he would say. This went on for ten years and finally on his 75th birthday, he succumbed to the pressure and agreed to reveal the secret. He said to an eager audience: "I never told a woman that my product would make her beautiful but I always gave her hope. Hope is the secret behind my formula."

Rabbi Hugo Gryson told of an experience when he and his father were in a Nazi concentration camp in 1944. On the feast of Hanukkah, his father secretly lit the Hanukkah lights using margarine and oil. And he protested saying: "Dad, why are you wasting food on a religious ritual?" His dad looked at him and said: "Son, we've often lived for as long as three weeks without food but we cannot possibly live for three minutes without hope."

Hope is one of those essentials invisible to the eye. It's one of those essentials that cannot be bought. It's true what the Rabbi's father said and what that cosmetic manufacturer saw as his secret formula. Hope is an ingredient that not only makes life whole but life can't be carried on without it.

Another one of those essentials invisible to the eye is generosity. A recent television documentary pointed out that the cheetah survives the African plains by running down its prey. The big cat

Life Injections IV

has been known to be able to sprint up to a speed of 70 miles an hour. The problem, however, is that if they don't run down their prey on their first burst of speed, they will never be able to catch up with them. And that's because they have a small heart and that small heart causes the cheetah to tire very quickly.

There are many people with small hearts and they, too, tire very quickly and that's because there's nothing driving them, there's nothing sustaining them, they have little to get excited about and they're supportive of no cause greater than themselves.

John Wesley, who was the spiritual father of the Methodist Church, did enough work to kill a hundred men. He got up at four o'clock in the morning and began preaching at five. He road up and down England on horseback in all kinds of weather. He would live to a ripe old age of 88. When he was asked as to the secret behind his energy, how he could maintain his rigorous schedule, how it was that he never looked tired, he pointed to his giving of himself for the cause of the gospel, he pointed, in essence, to his generosity.

And not only can generosity keep you from tiring, but it can keep you alive as well. Take that study conducted at the University of Michigan that followed 423 elderly couples for five years. It found that people who cared for others, people who were generous; they had a 60% lower rate of premature death than those who did not reach out at all to anyone, than those of whom it could be said that they had a small heart.

Generosity is but another on those essentials invisible to the eye, another one of those ingredients that makes life fruitful and whole. And so it can be said of meaning and purpose.

The late Leo Buscaglia liked to tell the story about a young girl who was walking through a meadow one day and saw a butterfly impaled upon a thorn. Very carefully and lovingly, she released the butterfly and it began to fly away. But then it came back and it changed into a fairy godmother. "Because you were kind of me," said the fairy godmother to that little girl, "I will grant you your fondest wish." The little girl thought for a moment and she said: "I want to be happy!" The fairy godmother leaned toward her and whispered something in her ear and suddenly vanished. As the girl grew older, she became happier and happier. No one else in the land was nearly as happy. But whenever anyone asked her for the secret of her happiness, she would only smile and say: "I listened to a good fairy godmother." As she reached the last years of her life, her neighbors became afraid that her fabulous secret for happiness would die with her. "Tell us," they said, "please tell us the secret of your happiness, and tell us what the good fairy godmother said." The lovely older lady warmly smiled and said: "The good fairy godmother whispered into my ear these words:" 'Everyone has need of you! No matter how secure they may seem, everyone has need of you!'"

There is nothing more vital to a person's life than feeling needed and that's best accomplished through a project or a service that contributes to the health and well being of the community; a project or a service where the helpless are helped, the poor are being cared for and the children are given the help and the guidance and the outlets they need to grow; a project or service that provides the giver with the sense that someone or something needs them.

The sense of being needed goes hand in hand with meaning and purpose and time and again it's been shown to be one of those essentials invisible to the eye, one of those ingredients that make life fruitful and whole.

And then there's the matter of fellowship. In the finest of infant homes of the 1800's, the mortality rate was over 70% and that was because their fear of spreading infection resulted in the infants being kept from human contact. That proved to be more deadly than any virus or disease. The lack of touch caused those infants to waste away showing how vital fellowship is, how vital human touch is to the health and well being of a child.

A study at John Hopkins University examined the health records of 1300 medical students over a period of eighteen years and it revealed that the strongest prognosticator for cancer, mental illness and the like was a lack of contact with family and a lack of contact with friends. Another study involving 7,000 people revealed that those with few close contacts tended to die two or three times sooner than those who saw their friends on a regular basis, than those in fellowship with more than just themselves.

Our life expectancy, the degree of health and well being we enjoy is more dependent on fellowship than the food we eat or the liquids we drink or the roof that may or may not lie above our heads. It's what makes fellowship one of those essentials invisible to the eye, one of those ingredients that make life fruitful and whole.

And, finally, there's what we call peace. The story goes that a woman longed to find out what paradise was like. She prayed constantly for this knowledge. One night, she had a dream. In the dream, an angel came and took her to heaven. They walked down a street and when they came to an ordinary looking house, the angel said: "Go and look inside!" She looked through a window and she saw a woman preparing dinner, another person reading the paper and children playing games. The woman turned to the angel and said: "Is this all there is to paradise?" The angel replied: "Those people you saw in the house are not in paradise, paradise is in them!"

People have paradise in them when they have peace in their soul. The peace of not having compromised their integrity. The peace of having sorted out well their priorities. The peace of having no regrets, the peace of having been honest and authentic and true to one's self.

When our souls are minus that peace, not only is paradise not within us but neither is the will to live. That's why peace is one of those essentials invisible to the eye, one of those ingredients that makes life fruitful and whole

I believe that we are by now familiar with the series of commercials put out by Master Card. Those commercials flash on the screen the cost of the various products and activities featured in the commercial. It comes to a close with the point as to how the cost of all those products and activities pale by comparison to the smile on someone's face or the joy in someone's soul and the good experience that was had which they tell you at the end is "priceless." And so it goes for all those essentials invisible to the eye, all those ingredients that make life fruitful and whole. They are priceless.

Our first reading today from Ecclesiastes warns us that all things are vanity while our Gospel laughs at the fool overly consumed with building barns for all his stuff. Saint Paul in our second reading put it best when he suggests we seek and set our sights on things from above. In other words, we seek and set our sights on what is invisible to the eye, on what is in fact priceless.

That story with which I began, the story of the woman who purchased the parrot at that local pet store, is a story it would do us well to heed. We're often buying mirrors by which to primp, ladders by which we try and climb higher, and swings upon which we seek pleasure. But if we neglect food for our souls, like that parrot, we too will perish.

My friends, set your sights on things from above! Set your sights on that which is priceless! Hold on to hope! Gain the feel that you are needed by seeking that which will put meaning and purpose in your life. Build up your energy and extend your life span by expanding your heart. Pursue the peace that will put paradise inside you. Multiply your friendships. Reach out in service to others. Do this and you'll have what it takes to make life fruitful and whole. You'll have what's essential yet invisible to the eye.

Siamese Twins

Luke 18: 9-14

"...O God I thank you that I am not like the rest of humankind..."

Problems ensue when we are not our real selves.

P. T. Barnum, the greatest showman who ever lived, once brought to this country a pair of Siamese twins. They traveled all over the United States as part of what Barnum called the greatest show on earth and they proved to be a major attraction to millions of wondering people. The Siamese twins were two young men who were joined together at the waist in such a manner that it would've meant death to separate them. So they had to live their lives as two men occupying one body and, at the time, it was the only case of its kind ever known. Its strangeness sparked a worldwide curiosity. How do they sleep? How do they eat? How do they go out? They were just a few of the questions circus patrons raised as they thought of the challenge of two individuals sharing one body, as they thought of two minds having one body to share between them.

We are all, of course, glad we are not Siamese twins. None of us, I believe, could fathom living with another person from whom we could never get away even for an instant. But if you think of it, if you give it some thought, some of us are in fact Siamese twins or even Siamese triplets or quadruplets. Some of us have living inside our one body a multitude of individuals taking turns occupying the one body they share between them. We may not be Siamese in the traditional sense of that term but we do come across as being more than one person, as two different people occupying one body. And when that's the case, when that's how we come across, there is much we stand to lose.

We first of all stand to lose our sincerity. There's a very odd bit of sculpture that adorns the grounds of Robinson Hall in Yorkshire England. It's what's commonly called the two-faced Butler. On one side there is a face that is all smiles. On the other side is a face with a scowl, a face resonating with insolence and impoliteness. It was commissioned by a leader of a prominent family who caught one of their butlers making rude and discourteous gestures the minute his head was turned. And what was particularly bothersome to that leader of that prominent family was that that very same butler was so kind and so generous when his back was not turned. He commissioned the sculpture as a warning that such behavior would not be tolerated.

I can't help but recall one of the iconic figures of my generation, that famous friend of Wally Cleaver, Eddie Haskell. Whenever Eddie was in the presence of Ward or June Cleaver, he could not have been more polite. He gushed with niceties and assorted compliments. And then, not unlike that butler after whom that statue was sculpted, the minute Ma and Pa Cleaver turned their back, the minute Eddie was out of earshot of Wally's parents, he'd return to being his usual smart aleck self who was anything but nice and anything but polite.

There are some of us who have a Siamese twin sharing the same body yet bearing little resemblance to whom we truly happen to be. If that twin takes control, it raises all kinds of questions in regards to our honesty. If our Siamese twin happens to be a phony, its sincerity, honesty and trust that we stand to lose.

And it can go badly as well if our Siamese twin is a chameleon. In his documentary movie, <u>Zelig</u>, Woody Allen portrays a man that was so afraid to offend anyone that he literally becomes a human chameleon. When he was in a New Orleans jazz band, he became black. When he was in a fat man's organization, he became fat. He visited China and became Chinese, visited Latin America and became Hispanic. The man had absolutely no identity of his own as he went to great lengths to be a part of whatever group that caught his fancy.

The documentary made for good comedy, but in its own way provided a parody of someone who can't assume self responsibility. Harriet Beecher Stowe once told of a party she went to where

Life Injections IV

everyone seemed to have left themselves at home. That's a pretty accurate assessment of what's commonly known as the cocktail circuit where identities are assumed based on the content of the conversation that happens to be going on. There are those who have a Siamese twin who shares the same body and who in chameleon fashion is constantly altering his or her identity, not wishing to claim a one as their own.

I remember reading of Carl Sandburg telling of a chameleon who made it just fine changing his colors to match the environment until one day he accidentally crawled into a Scotch plaid sports coat and had a nervous breakdown heroically trying to relate to everything at once.

Sandburg's comic tale applies to our oft found chameleon behavior. If our Siamese twin is a chameleon and it takes control, it can pose a serious threat to our stability. The people we may be trying to please can at times resemble that plaid sports coat and that can push our stress levels way beyond their danger zone. If our Siamese twin is a chameleon, we stand to lose our mind.

And it's authenticity we stand to lose if our Siamese twin is who we are supposed to be instead of who we are. I'll never forget a lecture we sponsored at Sisters Hospital some 20 years ago. The lecturer was Dr. Lew Forti and the audience were clergy from all sorts of denominations and from all across our community. Dr. Forti was talking about hospital visitation and he stressed the importance of clergy visiting their parishioners with no pretense. In other words, they were to just be there in their presence.

Well, that set off a firestorm amongst those attending the lecture. Clergy from both sides of the aisle, Catholic as well as Protestant, said that that would never do. They talked of people expecting them to say a prayer, expecting them to perform a ritual. That somehow they'd be shortchanging their parishioners if they were to just be themselves, if they didn't assume their clergy role.

Dr. Forti's point had been obviously missed. He was merely trying to tell them they should not enter a patient's room with an agenda, a checklist of clergy requirements. They should not enter a patient's room playing a role.

When I trained for chaplaincy, Dr. Forti's point was the entire essence of my training. The two units of CPE (Clinical Pastoral Education) all stressed Forti's key point which was how in hospital visitation we were to be in a patient's presence not as an actor, but as a real person concerned for their plight. In other words, at the bedside of someone who was sick, it was imperative for us to be who we are and not who we were supposed to be.

Father John Powell once told of a psychiatrist who could gain instant access to the deepest parts of anyone who came to him with a problem and it rested not on the questions he asked but on the person that he was: honest, open, and real.

I remember a nurse who thought she should quit her job in the nursery because when the mother of a baby who had just died appeared in the doorway, she, the nurse, broke into tears and cried uncontrollably in the mother's arms. The nurse felt that was unprofessional, unbecoming a nurse who was placed in charge of the nursery. When the time came for that mother to say goodbye, she couldn't say enough about the nurse who cried, she was beside herself in gratefulness for the genuineness that shined through her tears.

You see, that mother, at that time, needed not a professional relaying the facts but needed instead a caring individual very aware of the tragedy that had just unfolded and who showed it. If our Siamese twin is the person we're supposed to be and not the person who we are, and that twin takes control, it will cost us our authenticity and with it a chance for ministry in the true sense of that term.

So our Siamese twin can cost us sincerity, he or she can cost us peace of mind, he or she can cost us authenticity, or he or she can cost us the truth. A college recruiter heard good things about a high school basketball player from a small town. He got to the town too late for the game but was able to meet the young man and his coach. The recruiter said to the young man: "I hear you're pretty good!" "The best there is!" the player replied. "I average 45 points per game. I am the best rebounder in my school. And I've led our team to three undefeated seasons and three state championships." After talking to the player, he sought out his coach. The recruiter said to the coach: "The kid's a real talent! So tell me, does he have any weaknesses?" "Well," the coach said sheepishly. "He does have a tendency to exaggerate."

I'm reminded of that man and wife who were walking downtown. The man saw one of those machines that tell your fortune and your weight. He put in a coin and out came the little card and he began to read it. The card said: "You are a born leader; you have supreme intelligence, a quick wit and charming manners. You have a magnetic personality. You are highly attractive to the opposite sex." After reading the card, the man promptly handed it to his wife and said: "Take a look at this. Just read this card and see how lucky you are to have me as your husband." She read it and then turned it over and looked at the other side. She handed the card back to him and said: "It has your weight wrong too."

There's a part of us not unlike that high school star who loves to exaggerate, part of us, like that husband in the story I just told, who hold to an inflated version of whom they really are, a part of us like the Pharisee in today's Gospel who tend to think they're a cut above everyone else. When that part of us is our Siamese twin and he or she takes control, it will cost us the truth, the truth that can set us free from the illusion that may well have become our life.

My friends, we're all glad we are not Siamese twins. None of us could ever fathom living with another person from whom we could never separate even for an instant. But the fact is, the truth is, there are times when we are a Siamese twin or maybe even a Siamese triplet or quadruplet. There are times when inside us can be found a multitude of individuals taking turns occupying the one body they share between them. The good news, the great news is that if that's the case with us, we can separate. We can jettison those individuals none of whom happen to be our real self.

Our call today, God's call today is to be a Siamese twin or a Siamese triplet no longer. So, my friends, jettison all individuals that are not the real you. Jettison the Eddie Haskell part of you that's taken away your sincerity. Jettison the chameleon part of you that's robbed you of your peace of mind. Jettison the actor part of you that's stripped you of your authenticity. Jettison the Pharisee part of you, that's got you believing a lie. Get down to being one person and may that one person be the real you.

Hiss but Do Not Bite

John 2: 13-25

"...He made a whip out of cords and drove them out..."

How to handle anger.

A story is told of a snake that terrorized the children of a particular village whenever they went out to play. The elders of the village went and talked with the snake asking him to stop biting the children. The snake agreed and for the next several weeks the children played throughout the village without one word of complaint about the snake. So the elders decided to thank the snake for his cooperation and they went to see him only to find him battered and bruised and tied in knots. Asking what happened, the snake told how when he stopped biting the children, they began abusing him leaving him battered and bruised and tied in knots. The elders looked at the snake and said: "I'm sorry you misunderstood us. We asked you to stop biting the children. We didn't ask you to stop hissing."

It is hissing that I'd like to talk with you about today, not the hissing of a snake but the hissing that comes forth from you and me. Someone slights us and we hiss. Someone aggravates us and we hiss. Someone disrupts a perfectly wonderful day and we hiss.

Take the matter of shopping. The cart we grab keeps going in the wrong direction and the specials that brought us to the store in the first place have sold out. When we get to the express line, we discover that the person ahead has more than the ten items or less required at that register. A glance to our left reveals a cart filled with steak and lobster and other luxury items and a shopper with food stamps in hand. On our way to our parking spot, the bag rips and we come to find that someone parked so close that we can only enter our vehicle from the passenger side. A trip to the grocery store can often push our hisses to a level that could set off the seismograph at Canisius College.

Well, in case you haven't surmised, by hisses I mean anger, by hisses I mean rage. Of all the emotions we're capable of exhibiting, anger is by far, the one we exhibit the most. Rare is the person who doesn't register a high number on their anger index. And unfortunately, we've come to find that the greater the anger the greater the chance of someone getting hurt.

I remember reading with a chill a call that came to the emergency room of a hospital informing them that five persons were about to arrive, all in critical condition. Sadly, none of them survived and the cause of death was anger. The anger coming from a driver who recklessly passed a car that had ignited his rage triggering a two car accident that ended with those five people being killed.

Not only can someone get hurt from anger but hissing can be downright deadly and, as evidenced by that supermarket example, it doesn't take much and it doesn't take much time to get our blood to boil. That being said, what are we to do? What kind of options do we have when our hissing and anger and rage begin to rise? The first thing we can do is diffuse it.

Lincoln's Secretary of War, Edwin Stanton, was well known for his fits of rage and one day he went off in a rage about a general who really rattled his cage. Lincoln happened to be in earshot of Stanton's verbal assault and suggested that Stanton write that general a letter. "Tell him off with your pen!" said Lincoln. So Stanton sat down and began writing a scathing letter to the general, a letter in which he tore him to threads. He showed the letter to Lincoln and Lincoln called it first rate. "You really gave it to him!" But then he asked his Secretary of War as to what he was going to do with the letter and Stanton said he was going to mail it to the general. "Don't do that!" said Lincoln, "Put it in the stove and if you're still angry write another letter.

In a similar manner, the great Gandhi recommended to his grandson to keep an anger journal so that he might pour his anger onto a page instead of onto a person. Thomas Jefferson used to say that when you're angry count to ten before you speak and if very angry, count to 100. Mark Twain said that when angry count to four and when very angry swear. Athendorus Ananira, who died 80 years after the death of Christ, suggested that when we're angry we are not to say or do anything until we've recited the alphabet at least once. So the first thing to do when our anger and hissing and rage begins to rise is diffuse it, to find a way to keep it from having us say or do what we will afterwards regret.

The second thing we can do is find a way to properly direct it. Doctor Ralph Stockman tells of those early days of motion pictures when western thrillers were shown in the ranch towns of the west. The cowboys rode in from miles around and sat down in dingy movie theaters to watch the villain as he moved across the screen shooting up the town, robbing banks, and holding the lovely heroine hostage. It is said that the cowhands became so excited and so enraged at the villain that they'd stand up pull out their guns and begin shooting at the screen seemingly unaware that what they damaged was the movie furniture, not the villain. He was somewhere else.

All too often we'll get angry and enraged at people for what they do when in fact the real villain is somewhere else, when in fact they wouldn't be doing what they are doing if it were not for the horrible environment in which they live, if not for the abusive household from which they came, if not for the ignorance which had them engaging in abhorrent behavior. All too often when we direct our anger at people, we are not much better than those cowboys directing their guns at the silver screen.

I can't help but once again cite Candy Lightner, who when her daughter was killed by a drunk driver, directed her anger not at the driver but instead directed it to the laws and practices which allowed drivers like him to drive with impunity.

It would do us well to direct our anger not at bad people but to direct it instead at what it was that made them bad, to direct it at the poverty or the sin or the human misery that may have bred the badness.

The third thing we can do when our anger, our hissing, our rage begins to rise is to harness it. The Congressional Medal of Honor was given to a young officer who, when the battle looked hopeless, waged what his superior officers called a one man war. He took matters into his own hands and did the fighting of a hundred men. When asked how he did it, he replied: "I just got mad!"

A female volunteer at a retirement center saw the way elderly people were getting treated and she got mad. The result was her attending law school at the age of 62 and, upon passing the bar, advocating for the rights of senior citizens everywhere. Hospitals were horrible places until Florence Nightingale got mad. In her biography, she is presented not as a gentle angel of mercy but as a hot house of emotion, as an angry woman with the call of God within her soul, who hounded and bullied government officials into providing decent treatment for the wounded and the dying.

English prisons were the perfect picture of a vial, disease ridden hell on earth until John Howard and his followers got mad. The anger of Lincoln brought on the Emancipation Proclamation while the anger of Martin Luther King Jr. spawned the civil rights movement. What distinguished Lincoln and King and Howard and Nightingale and the Congressional Medal of Honor winner and the 62 year old lawyer was their ability to harness their anger, their ability to apply its tremendous power towards the ending of a wrong or the establishment of a right. Many positive things have come to pass thanks to people harnessing their anger and then applying it towards a good cause.

The fourth thing we can do when our hissing, anger and rage begins to rise is to assume the responsibility attached to it. You might remember that famous line from the old "Pogo" comic strip which read: "We have met the enemy and it is us!" Now that line often applies to our anger. We will say: "You made me angry!" when in fact no one can make us angry, that if our blood is boiling over someone's indiscretion, the anger problem lies with us and not with them All too often, when it comes to anger, "We have met the enemy and it is us."

And alongside this taking of responsibility for our anger is our taking responsibility for doing something about what it is that we happen to be angry about. I always liked that story of the priest who was walking on a dark and lonely street when he saw a pitiful human being lying in a gutter. His faith was suddenly shaken and he cried out: "O God, do you exist, are you there, do you care?"

And then with anger in his voice he shouts: "Why don't you do something about this pathetic soul?" He then hears a voice booming from the heavens. It's the voice of God saying: "I do exist and I do care and I am doing something about it. I've called him to your attention!"

So the question is: Are we just going to sit there and feel angry or are we going to get off our duffs and start doing something about what it is that's angering us. With anger comes responsibility, not only the responsibility of owning it as our problem but also the responsibility of acting on what it is that God's called to our attention.

The fifth thing we can do when our hissing, anger and rage begins to rise is to pray. The Psalms have taught us that it is not only safe but an extremely important duty and therapy to tell God about how angry and fed up we really feel at certain junctures in our life. Christ, himself, did as much when, upon hanging from the cross; he uttered the words of Psalm 22 with its haunting cry of anger and anguish: "O God, my God, why have you forsaken me!" So besides our diffusing our anger, our redirecting our anger, our harnessing our anger, our assuming the responsibilities of anger, we can always funnel it into prayer.

We read in today's Gospel of Jesus getting angry with the money changers at the temple. We read not long ago of Jesus hissing at Peter telling him: "Get behind me, Satan!" We've heard on several occasions of Jesus growing angry at the hypocrisy of the Pharisees. St. Paul in many of his letters writes about his anger. So we can surmise from all of that that anger is not a sin. The sin lies in what we do with the anger. Ala the snake in my opening story, it isn't the hissing that's the problem, it's the biting.

So my friends, as St. Paul admonished: "Be angry but do not sin!" Hiss all you want but do not bite. That means if you feel your hissing and your anger and your rage beginning to rise, diffuse it. Count to ten or pour your anger into an anger journal before you say or do a thing. Direct it properly so it's pointed not at the villain but at the evil responsible for the villain. Follow the lead of the Nightingale's and Lincoln's and have something good come from it. Take responsibility for it. Don't blame it on others and be sure you don't just feel the anger but you also do something about what it's called to your attention.

Watchmen and Watchwomen

Ezekiel 33: 7-9

"...I have appointed watchmen for the house of Israel..."

The special people who helped us and the world to realize a better day.

I've always been a big fan of science fiction and so I've gotten to enjoy a program on the Fox network called *The Fringe*. Not unlike the X-Files of long ago, it revolves around a law enforcement agency, specifically the FBI, in particular what's called its fringe division. It features an archetypical mad scientist Dr.Walter Bishop, Peter Bishop, Walters's estranged son who is a Jack of all trades, and agents Olivia Dunham and Astrid Farnsworth. Their job is to investigate strange and unusual happenings.

On the program from time to time, you'll encounter a mythical group of men, who are bald, who usually wear a suit and a hat. They lack facial hair of any kind and they frequently display socially peculiar behavior. They've been known to live for centuries as they can be seen in photographs of important moments in modern human history. That mythical group of men are called "Observers" and although the exact nature of their mission has never been explained[16], they appear to be observing all the goings-on in the world with the intention of making sure that everything goes on as planned, making sure that everything goes on in the way in which it was intended.

It's "observers" I'd like to talk with you about today, not the "observers" in that science-fiction sitcom, but those who could be seen as observers, watchmen as they're called in today's first reading. Ezekiel outlines their duty as watching over the house of Israel and down through the years there've been many a watchman, many a watchwoman who not only watched over the house of

Israel but they watched over the world. And in so doing, they did their best, they sacrificed, they put their life and their well being on the line, they did what they could, often at great risk, all in response to what they had been watching, all in reaction to what they had seen and observed. And the world and us have been the better because of it.

I remember reading the story of a hero of the Chinese rice fields in the aftermath of an earthquake. One day when the sky was like thunder, he saw from his hilltop farm that the ocean was suddenly receding like an animal crouching to leap and he knew the leap would be a tidal wave and that his neighbors working in the low fields would be swept away by raging waters. Without a second thought, he set fire to his own rice field and furiously rang the Temple Bell. His neighbors saw his farm on fire and rushed up to help. Then from that safe height, they saw the wall of water overtaking the fields they had vacated and they knew that they had been saved at great cost to their "Savior." That farmer saw and observed an impending disaster and he gave up his farm, gave up his livelihood for the sake of those upon whom that disaster would unfold.

You might recall my telling you of Ignaz Semmelweis, a Hungarian obstetrician, who happened to see and observe the high mortality rates of mothers who delivered children. He concluded that some invisible substance was responsible and wondered if the physician might be the carrier of that substance. He instructed the physicians under his charge to wash their hands before every delivery. As a result, the mortality rate for expectant mothers in his hospital dropped substantially. When he tried to get word out to the medical establishment as to what he had seen and observed, when he tried to warn doctors as to their unsafe practices, he met with a resistance that was so vitriolic that it took its toll on Semmelweis to the point where his reputation and mental well-being were severely damaged.

Sometimes a watchman, sometimes a watchwoman takes on the form of that farmer or that Hungarian obstetrician where they see and observe something dangerous and pay a heavy price for sounding the alarm, where they see and observe what eluded the eyes of others, and at great cost, try to help those others see and observe what they've missed. I envision here scientists, researchers, physicians and community leaders calling attention to practices and behavior detrimental to us and the world in which we live.

And sometimes that watchman, that watchwoman, that observer takes on the form of a coach, a teacher, a friend or a mentor. Some of you might recall a whimsical tale that made its way onto the silver screen. It featured a star-studded cast that included Will Smith, Chalize Teron, Matt Damon and Jack Lemmon. It was called *The Legend of Bagger Vance*. It centered around a two-day golf exhibition in Savanna, Georgia involving legendary golfers Bobby Jones and Walter Hagan and a former hometown golfing great Rannulph Junuh. Junuh, played by Matt Damon, had Tiger Woods level promise but after his World War I tour of duty, lost his interest in golf and became a recluse with gambling and heavy drinking occupying most of his time. The golf match was to be his path to redemption.

Bagger Vance, played by Will Smith, mysteriously appears in the dead of night while Junuh is hitting golf balls. He announces to him that he was to be his caddie. Bagger Vance becomes, instead, his Redeemer as throughout the golf exhibition he helped him regain his passion for the game as well as his passion for life, held him steady through a potential meltdown, challenged Junuh to do what's right when his integrity was being severely challenged. Bagger Vance would mysteriously exit Junuh's life just as he had mysteriously entered it.

Many a life has been the beneficiary of a Bagger Vance, beneficiary of a person who observes and sees their failings, observes and sees their destructive habits, observes and sees their lapse in integrity, observes and sees their inability to reach their potential; and that he or she then steps forward and a change occurs, redemption is realized, what was lost gets found and life is reborn.

I'm referring to teachers, advisors, mentors, coaches who see and observe our behavior and thanks to their rebuke, thanks to their counsel, thanks to their affirmation; we were spared a miserable life, we were steered away from a negative direction, we found the life we were meant to live. Many of us have been fortunate to have a watchman or a watchwoman of the ilk of a Bagger Vance enter into our life.

And than you have watchmen, watchwomen of the ilk of a visionary who sees into the future and acts in that accord. I recently ran across this wonderful poem:

> An old man, going a lone highway,
> Came at the evening, cold and gray,
> To chasm, vast and deep and wide,
> Through which was flowing a sullen tide.
> The old man crossed in the twilight dim;
> The sullen stream had no fears for him;
> But he turned when safe on the other side
> And built a bridge to span the tide.
>
> "Old man," said a fellow pilgrim near,
> "You are wasting strength with building here;
> Your journey will end with the ending day;
> You never again must pass this way;
> You have crossed the chasm, deep and wide—
> Why build you a bridge at the eventide?"
>
> The builder lifted his old gray head:
> "Good friend, in the path I have come," he said,
> "There followeth after me today
> A youth whose feet must pass this way.
> This chasm that has been naught to me
> To that fair-haired youth may a pitfall be,
> He, too, must cross in the twilight dim;
> Good friend, I'm building the bridge for him."

I'm reminded of that wonderful story by Jean Giono entitled: *The Man Who Planted Hope and Grew Happiness* [17]. The man in the story was a Frenchman who lived in southwest France in the early 20th century. He lived alone in a barren area that had once been a forest with its own village. His life was simple. He went out each day and planted trees. Year after year, decade after decade, seed by seed, he kept planting. The trees began to grow into a forest which held water in the soil so that other plants could grow, birds could make nests, streams could flow and families could return and build houses. What had once been a village was a village once again. By the end of his lifetime, he had totally transformed and restored the natural environment of an entire region.

You could well call that old man in that poem and the Frenchman in that story watchmen who saw and observed what the future needed, whose eyes peered well beyond the present world to a world better and prettier than ours. And with that, they took it upon themselves to see to it that the better and prettier world came to pass.

So you have watchmen and watchwomen like Semmelweis and that Chinese farmer who see and observe danger and then pay a price for sounding the alarm. You have watchmen, watchwomen like Bagger Vance who see and observe our failing ways and steer us in an opposite direction. You have watchmen, watchwomen like that Frenchman and that bridge builder who see and observe well into the future and act in that accord. Then you have watchmen, watchwomen who've taken the role of a prophet.

Some of the great players the sports world has ever known were gifted with breadth of vision. Legendary Bob Cousy was tested for this and it was found his peripheral vision was about 50% greater than the average person. Some said Bob Cousy could look due east and enjoy a sunset.

The same is true with Bill Bradley. When Bradley played for Princeton, he was taken to an ophthalmologist and tested for peripheral vision and it was found that Bradley had peripheral vision about 40% greater than the average person. Bradley had been known for his ability to throw the ball to a teammate when he wasn't looking in his direction. People claim Bradley had eyes in the back of his head.

It was said of Wayne Gretzky, arguably the greatest hockey player ever that he could see all over the ice. That gift of vision, that breadth of vision has not only been in evidence in the greats of the sports world, but it's been in evidence as well in the prophets of the world, men and women who call attention to a truth we fail to see, men and women who bring to our awareness issues and concerns of a much larger nature and with greater ramifications than the issues and concerns that occupy our attention. There are

Life Injections IV

many a watchman, many watchwoman who use their Cousy, Bradley and Gretzky vision to prophesy as to what we should be worried about, as what we should be concerned about and doing something about if, in fact, we are claiming to be a member of the Body of Christ.

Ezekiel in our first reading tells of appointing a watchman for the house of Israel whose duty it was to warn them of their sinful ways. We may not know of any official appointment to be a watchman or watchwoman but they're most assuredly in our midst. It may have been that someone who saw danger looming in our life or in our world and sounded the alarm, that someone who saw we needed guidance or encouragement or redemption and proceeded to deliver it, that someone who saw what a future world needed and put in place what we'd later enjoy, that someone who saw how trivial and selfish were our concerns and worries and called us to a broader vision of life with the duties and obligations and worries which that vision entails.

I'm not sure if the sitcom Fringe will ever let us know the real story behind the "Observers." But I am sure that God has provided us with observers, watchmen and watchwomen and the story may well be that God's looking to us to assume that appointment, looking to us to see and observe for someone or for the world what would be to their benefit.

If Disillusionment Comes Your Way

Hebrews 12: 18-19, 22-24

"...you have approached Mt Zion...and countless angels in festal gathering..."

What to keep in mind should you become disillusioned.

Disillusionment reigns supreme in these days and times in which we live. Whether it be John Edward's sordid affair in the world of politics or the Tiger Woods saga in the world of golf or the pedophile scandal in the world of the Catholic Church or the Michael Vick and Ben Rothlesberger stories in the world of football or the John and Kate breakup in the world of television or Mel Gibson's meltdown in the world of Hollywood; fallen idols litter the landscape of almost every institution in this land of ours. Mix into that the bickering and the vitriol on both sides of the political aisle and mix into that the bad economy and it could well be said there's much to be disillusioned about.

That being so, I'd like to talk with you today about disillusionment, talk with you about some things to consider should you be disillusioned about your life or disillusioned about the world or disillusioned about the happenings going on around you.

First of all, you need to consider the source. During a recent five-year period, homicides across our country decreased by 13% while, during that same time, coverage of homicides on the three major television networks increased by 336%. While public safety has actually improved, the media makes it appear that it's gotten worse.

The media as a general rule feeds on the negative. As the old adage goes, if it bleeds it leads.

A radio talk show host once put it best when he described the news as a proctological view of life and by that he meant that most of the news reported as the events of the day represent the sewage portion of what actually went on that day. Just as the garbage in our trash is not a fair representation of our life, so is the daily news not a fair representation of life on this planet.

Several years ago, the Saturday Evening Post ran a cartoon showing a man about to be rescued after he spent a long time shipwrecked on a tiny deserted island. The sailor in charge of the rescue team stepped onto the beach and handed the man a stack of newspapers. "Compliments of the Captain," the sailor said, "he would like you to glance at the headlines to see if you still would like to be rescued."

Whether it be the evening news on television or the contents of your daily newspapers or the banter of talk show hosts on the radio, the sewage of life gets far more play than the positive things of life. What's usually talked about or reported about or sensationalized is but a tiny portion of the happenings of a given day.

The Jesuit Anthony De Mello once told of a factory that was interested in buying bullfrog skins. A farmer wired the company claiming he could supply any quantity, 200,000 and more on-demand. The company wired back: "Send the first consignment of 50,000." Two weeks later one single pathetic frog skin came through the mail with this note "Sirs, I apologize; this is all the frog skins that were available in the neighborhood. The noise certainly fooled me."

If you are disillusioned about the goings-on of the world at large or the world around you, consider the source; don't let its negative voice fool you. Don't let a proctological view of life be the lens through which you view the world.

And besides considering the source of our disillusionment, we need to consider as well the company we keep. The story goes that a little boy was trying to raise some money going door-to-door in his neighborhood. He came upon the house of the woman known to be the town grouch. When she came to the door, the boy asked if she had any old coke bottles and with a rough voice she bellowed No! He then asked if she had any old whiskey bottles. She looked at him angrily and said: "Young man! Do I look like the kind of person who would have a lot of old whiskey bottles?" He studied her for a moment and said "No, ma'am, you're right. But I bet you have a lot of old vinegar bottles."

Vinegar people abound in the world in which we live and if an over preponderance of our friends are of that ilk, it's going to be hard for us not to be disillusioned. It's going to be hard for us not to have a negative view of life.

John Tyndale, the famous physicist, once referenced an old mariner practice called shooting the sun. On a regular basis, the ship's captain would shoot the sun which meant he'd check the ship's clocks and charts by taking a fresh observation of the ship's position in regards to the sun. Tyndale then warned us as to how we should never garner an opinion or make a decision or assess a situation if there happens to be dark clouds all around us. Like a ship's captain, we should only do so when the sun is visible for it's only then that we can get a proper read and attain the proper bearings when it comes to life.

If the company we keep consists of vinegar people, if dark clouds hover around those we are close to and near, we are not able to shoot the sun and so the disillusionment we feel may well be the result of an improper read of life, the result of our not having the proper bearings as to where life is and where life is going.

Besides considering the source or considering the company we keep, another thing to consider should disillusionment come our way is that perhaps our eggs were placed in the wrong basket. I know someone who bought a beautiful home in an upscale neighborhood. He was happy until he moved in. The thrill was then gone and he wished he bought a bigger home. I read about an actor who received $1 million for every film he made. He was unhappy because Arnold Schwarzenegger was making one million more. It's been said that when Forbes magazine lists the 400 wealthiest people, many a wealthy soul grows very upset because it acknowledges the fact that there are people wealthier than they.

These are extreme cases but the folks I've just mentioned are but a microcosm of a number of people who've grown disillusioned because they thought that the betterment of themselves financially, the ability to realize all their wants and needs, they thought it would render them peace. They thought it would end their problems. They thought it would provide them happiness when in fact it did none of the above. Had they placed their eggs in the right basket, had they set their priorities straight when it comes to what's important, they wouldn't have been so disillusioned.

Another thing to consider should disillusionment come our way is our mindset, what we expect when it comes to life. C.S. Lewis tells us that the world is like a building. Half the people who live in it think it's a prison while the rest believe it to be a five-star hotel. Those who think it is a prison cannot get over how good things are, while those who think it a hotel are constantly complaining about the room service.

A lot of our disillusionment may well be generated by the nature of our expectations, how we expect life to be. If we expect life to be a bowl of cherries, if we expect goodness to be rewarded and sin to be punished or justice to be served; we're going to be disillusioned because a five-star hotel life is not.

Life may not be a prison in the exact sense of that term but life does have its share of cruelties, its share of injustices, its share of pain. There may well be occasions where we find ourselves in pain or find ourselves a victim of injustice, or we find ourselves living under less than ideal conditions. If our expectations account for that fact, there's less of a chance of our being disillusioned because we'll realize and understand that life doesn't always turn out the way we had hoped that it would.

I like that story of David, the second-grader, who was bumped while getting on a school bus resulting in a two inch cut on his cheek. At recess, he collided with another boy and lost two teeth. At noon, while sliding on the ice, he fell and broke his wrist and got taken to the hospital. When his father arrived, he finds David with a big smile on his face. He's holding onto a quarter in his good hand and he says to his dad: "I found this quarter on the ground when I fell. It's the first-quarter I ever found. This sure is my lucky day."

You might say that boy expected life to serve up two inch cuts and lost teeth and broken wrists. You could say, in C.S. Lewis' terms, that he thought life to be a prison. Because he did, the bad things didn't phase him. He was tickled pink about the quarter he found. It made his day.

Expectations determine disillusionment. If we expect life to be a bowl of cherries, if we expect life to be a five-star hotel, we're going to be disillusioned rather easily. If we expect life to have its hard and difficult times, if we expect life to be a prison, we'll not be disillusioned easily and, when something good comes our way, we'll beam with joy.

And just as expectation determines disillusionment, so does attitude. I loved the story of the 92-year-old woman moving into a nursing home. Since she was legally blind and her husband of seventy years had passed away, there was no other option. She waited in the lobby of the nursing home for a long time before her room was ready. As she was escorted down the corridor, her attendant described the room right down to the curtains hanging on the window. "I love it!" the elderly lady enthusiastically said. "But ma'am, you haven't seen the room yet!" the attendant cautioned. "It doesn't matter," she said. "Whether I like my room or not is not dependent upon how the furniture is arranged. It's dependent upon how I've arranged my mind."

Not unlike expectation, how we arrange our minds determines our disillusionment. Recall here that old Robert Browning couplet: "Two men looked out the prison bars; one saw mud the other saw stars!" Our vision, our attitude, the arrangement of our minds can well determine our disillusionment when it comes to what may be sitting before our eyes.

The last thing to consider should disillusionment come our way is that God may well be near. Our reading from Hebrews today speaks to that. The author of the selection from Hebrews says that when we approach hard times and bad times, the storm, the fire, gloomy darkness, as he called it; we're actually approaching Mt. Zion. There, as he put it, will be found countless angels in festal gathering, with the assembly of the firstborn enrolled in heaven and with God, with Jesus, embracing us. In other words, disillusionment can be our avenue to God.

My friends, should disillusionment come your way, first of all consider the source. Consider the fact that the media presents us with a proctological view of life. Consider the company you keep. Don't let the vinegar people sour you. Consider your expectation of life. Remember a five-star hotel life is not. Consider as to whether you placed your eggs in the right basket. Consider how you've arranged your mind. And finally consider the fact of God's presence. God's felt as you have felt. God's been where you have been. And your experience brings you closer to God than you've ever been before.

Just Do It

Luke 16: 1-13

"...And the master commended that dishonest steward for acting prudently..."

The positive spin on a difficult Gospel.

A young salesman approached a farmer and began to talk excitedly about the book he happened to be selling. "This book," he says to the farmer, "this book tells you everything you need to know about farming. It tells you when to sow and when to reap. It tells you about the weather, what to expect and when to expect it. It tells you about crop rotation and the tilling of the soil. This book tells you all you need to do to run a successful farm." "Young man," said the farmer, "I'm not about to buy your book. You see I know all about what's inside it. I know all there is to know about farming. I know all you need to do to run a successful farm. My problem is doing it."

It's doing it that I'd like to talk with you about today. It's taking action that I'd like to discuss with you today. Unfortunately, far too many of us know what we need to do. We know the action we need to take. But like that farmer, our problem is doing it. Our problem is taking action. And the fact is that if we ever did do it, if we ever did take action, there would be much that we'd stand to gain.

First of all, we'd stand to gain relief from needless suffering. I'm reminded of the story of the dog sitting on a porch moaning and groaning. A man walks by and asks the owner of the house why the dog was moaning and groaning and the owner replies that it's because he's lying on a nail. "If that's the case," the man inquired, "why doesn't he get off the nail?" "Well," said the owner, "he's not hurting badly enough."

I believe we know a lot of people like that dog on that porch. They're constantly complaining, they're constantly moaning about their lot in life, they're constantly proclaiming how bad things happen to be. But because the situation isn't desperate, because they're still able to function, because it is not hurting bad enough, they never move off the nail. And the sad truth is that their pain can be remedied, their hurt can be fixed, their misery can end, but it's going to take some doing, it's going to take some action. But since that's not in the cards at the moment, they moan and groan and keep lying upon the nail.

So the first gain, the first perk from our doing something, from our taking action is relief from needless suffering. The second perk, the second gain is credibility. The great preacher Halford Luccock wrote a book which was a compilation of humorous articles he had written for Christian Century Magazine. In one of those columns he did a takeoff on the famous line: "His bark is worse than his bite!" He wrote to advocate for the opposite. He wrote that what we need most are public speakers and political figures whose bite is worse than their bark. As he saw it, too many public speakers and political figures do a tremendous amount of barking, they do a tremendous amount of talking with little to show for any of it. Luccock mused as to how it would be so much better if they did less barking and more biting, if they talked less and did more.

I think here of Dwight C. Moody, the famous Biblical scholar who was crucified mercilessly about the way he evangelized and Moody asked his critic how he happened to evangelize only to have the critic admit that he didn't evangelize at all. That prompted Moody to say: "Look, Mister, I prefer my way of doing it to your way of not doing it."

Without a doubt, there are many people like that critic of Moody. Big on barking and light on biting; big on talking, light on doing; big on promising, light on delivering on the promise. There is no greater source of credibility than the backing of words with action, no greater avenue to trustworthiness than to be found doing something about what fueled our barking.

So our doing it, our taking action can provide relief from needless suffering, it can insure credibility, and third, it can provide peace of mind.

A man once came to a farmer and asked to be taken in as a hired hand. "What can you do?" the farmer asked him. He replied: "I can sleep well on a windy night." The farmer found that an odd reply, but needing an extra worker, he hired him. Soon thereafter, the farmer went out of town and the night on which he happened to return was a night from hell as a thunderstorm ushered in gale force winds. The farmer panicked. He remembered the broken barn door, the weak spot in the fence, and the ripped wire in the chicken coop and figured the winds did them in and he feared that his horses and cattle and chickens had by now escaped into the night. He runs to the barn only to find that the barn door had been fixed. He hustles to the fence only to find that it's been repaired. And when he got to the chicken coop, he saw that the ripped wire was ripped no more. Finding his hired hand fast asleep, he came to realize what the man had meant when he said he could sleep well on a windy night. His having taken action on the farm's needed repairs meant that he'd have nothing to worry about should a storm occur and, being thus free of worry, he could sleep rather well.

There are many people who do not sleep well because they are very anxious and worried over matters and concerns which should have been handled and dealt with a long time past. Had they done something about them, had they taken action on their resolution, they'd have had the peace of mind necessary for a restful sleep.

I like what that old Jewish Rabbi said when his student asked him as to when was the best time to repent. He answered by saying that one should always repent on the last day of one's life. The student then remarked as to how one could never be certain as to when would be the last day of their life. "Therefore," said the Rabbi, "you had best repent today!" So the fact is we need to take action when it comes to resolving problems, when it comes to repairing broken friendships, when it comes to seeking forgiveness, and when it comes to repenting. Delaying that action not only makes for sleepless nights but for plenty of regrets and a great deal of remorse.

And besides peace of mind, doing and taking action can also assure a clear conscience. In law books, you will find the expression accessory before the fact as well as accessory after the fact. If a person helps bank robbers get away, he or she is guilty as an accessory after the fact. If he or she helps to plan the robbery but takes no part in it or if he or she knows it's coming to pass and does not act on that knowledge, he or she is guilty as an accessory before the fact.

With every great world tragedy, there are many accessories before the fact, there are many people who are guilty, many who are responsible in the degree to which they might have done something to prevent it, but in fact did nothing. When we fail to do anything, when we fail to take any sort of action on something which we know in our heart of hearts we should have done something about; we may very well find ourselves an accessory before the fact. We may well find ourselves being remorseful and regretful as some bad thing occurs which we had it in our power to stop. If we want a clear conscience, then it's imperative that we not sit back and do nothing when we know there's something which we can and should do.

And besides assuring us a clear conscience, our doing, our taking action can also assure us of respect and admiration. There was a sickly child named Theodore whom other boys had a habit of pushing around. After being thrashed by a neighborhood bully, Theodore decided to do something about it. He decided to get tough, to work hard and train so he'd be strong enough to stand up to all and anyone who tried to bully him. Theodore's last name was Roosevelt.

When Handel's health and fortune reached their lowest ebb, when it appeared as though his whole world was caving in around him, it was then that he composed his greatest work: the Messiah.

When John Bunyan was at his lowest, when he was stuck in a jail, it was then that he wrote his greatest work: Pilgrim's Progress.

Some of the most respected and admired of individuals that history has ever produced earned that admiration and respect because when they had every right to sit back and be bitter; when they had every right to sit back and wallow in their misery, they embarked instead upon an action to help dispel the darkness that enveloped their life.

So when life is not treating us well, when we're in the throws of some awful and miserable experience, we are afforded the same choice as was afforded Roosevelt, Handel, and Bunyan. We can sit back or we can take action. We can whine or we can do something which may well earn us the respect and admiration of many.

And, finally, our doing, our taking action assures us of popularity. Journalist Leo Aikman said there are four kinds of bones in every organization. First, there are the wishbones who see the problem, talk about it, and then hope and wish that someone would do something about it. Second, you have the jawbones who see the problem, talk about it incessantly but do little else. Third, you have the knucklebones who see the problem, talk it to death and then criticize whatever is being done about it. And fourth, you have the backbones who see the problem, study it carefully, and then they roll up their sleeves and do what needs to be done. I needn't tell you as to who happens to be the most popular of all the bones in an organization. It's, of course, the backbones. Doing, taking action, will assure you popularity in any business, any club, any church, and any community to which you may happen to belong.

Today's Gospel parable poses a problem for many because it has Jesus seemingly condoning dishonest behavior. It has Jesus acclaiming a manager who by changing the invoices was in effect cheating his boss. What we need to understand is that Jesus is not condoning the dishonesty or the cheating; he's recognizing instead the positive fact that the manager did something, he took action. In essence, by virtue of the parable, Jesus is calling on us to be doers, to be people who take action. And we, if we follow that call, have many perks awaiting us.

First of all, we'll gain relief from needless suffering by pulling ourselves off the nail we're lying upon. Second, we'll gain credibility, we'll be known for our bite instead of our bark. Third, we'll have peace of mind, we'll be able to sleep on a windy night. Fourth, we'll have a clear conscience. We won't be accused of being an accessory before the fact. Fifth, we'll gain respect and admiration for like Handel and Roosevelt and Bunyan, we won't sit back and whine when life hasn't worked out in the way that it should, Sixth, we'll be very popular because we'll be seen as the backbone of our organization.

The Nike Sneaker People have a phrase we see in every one of their commercials. That phrase is "Just Do It!" It was stolen from today's Gospel parable. If there is something in your life that you need to do something about, quit stalling, just do it!

Amplius

1 Corinthians 10:16-17
"...We, though many, are one body..."

We need to think bigger and to ponder greater things.

It is said that one day the great artist Michelangelo went into the studio of Raphael. He looked at one of his early drawings and considered it for a moment and then took a piece of chalk and wrote the word amplius across the entire drawing, amplius which means bigger or larger. Michelangelo was encouraging Raphael to magnify his work, to think bigger thoughts, to ponder greater things.

Well, it's amplius that I'd like to talk with you about today, it's thinking bigger and pondering greater things I'd like to discuss with you today. All too often our focus is narrow, all too often we tend to think and ponder in a very tiny and limited way.

There was a book written many years ago entitled *The Rosary* [18] The heroine of that bestseller was the Hon. Jane Chapman who had come upon hard times, her nerves having gotten the best of her. A Dr. Deryck Brand came upon the scene. When he saw how frayed her nerves had become, he immediately wrote a prescription. The prescription read: "See a few big things." What the doctor wanted her to do was to go and see Niagara Falls, or the skyscrapers of New York City, or the pyramids of Egypt. It was his belief that her coming face-to-face with such immense creations would cause her to realize just how small and minor were the worries and concerns that so upset her life.

Now, I realize we're talking fiction here but I believe Dr. Deryck Brand was onto something with his prescription because many times when we're provided with a bigger picture, when we're provided with a much larger perspective, our worries and concerns can appear very minor. Our worries and concerns may even appear to be petty and a cause for embarrassment that we had them at all.

And the good thing is that we don't need to see the pyramids or skyscrapers for that to happen. All we need do is to take a walk through an oncology ward or a walk through an intensive care unit of a Children's Hospital and it will hit us that compared with those of a cancer patient, when compared with those of parents living with the fear that their child may not see the light of another day, our worries and concerns appear very small. Thinking bigger and pondering greater can be a help when it comes to the worries and concerns that comes life's way. It can provide needed perspective.

And thinking bigger and pondering greater can be a help as well when it comes to the drudgery and the monotony that may be our work. British author Bernard Newman tells somewhere of his being in the home of a peasant family in a remote village in the Balkans. The daughter in the home he was visiting was spending hours upon hours, almost her entire day, sewing. Inquiring as to how she wasn't bored, how she wasn't tired stitching away her day, she replied: "I'm not bored and I'm not tired at all. You see I'm sewing my wedding dress." The difference between her sewing being a drudgery or a joy had to do with the bigger picture.

I'm reminded here of that often told story, often attributed to the great architect Christopher Wren, where he allegedly walked through the worksite of the building of Chartres Cathedral. He runs into a mason and he asks him: "What do you do?" And he says: "What does it look like? I'm laying brick." He walks further inside and encounters a glassblower. He asks him: "What do you do?" And he replied that he's making windows. Walking even deeper into the worksite, he encounters a woman sweeping up the dust and the glass chards and the broken pieces of brick. And he asked her: "What do you do?" She leans on her broom, looks up at the unfinished pillars and walls, and then she says to Christopher Wren: "What do I do? I'm building a cathedral for the honor and the glory of God."

Thinking bigger and pondering greater can often be a difference maker between drudgery and joy, between boredom and excitement. No matter what work it is we do or what job it is we have, it's a piece of a bigger picture. Sweeping, sewing, painting, writing, licking envelopes, driving buses, checking gauges, tightening screws can be awfully monotonous and can be a drudgery and in some cases even touted as a nothing job. But if you think big and ponder great, you may well see that what you are doing is a vital part of a bigger whole, a vital piece of a beautiful mosaic. And if you're doing what you are doing to the best of your ability, you'll also see it as doing something beautiful for God.

And thinking bigger and pondering greater can also expose prejudice. I can remember an interview some reporter had with the late Carl Sandburg. "Mr. Sandburg," he said, "you are a man of words. You've written poetry and history and biography. You write songs. As a man of words, what to you is the ugliest word in English language?" Sandburg was in his 80s, a shock of white hair fell upon his brow. He looks at the reporter and said: "The ugliest word? I believe the ugliest word to be the word exclusive."

Thinking bigger and pondering greater helps us to see that men do not have the market cornered when it comes to certain talents and abilities; to see that women do not have the market cornered when it comes to feminine qualities; to see that Christians do not have the market cornered when it comes to grace; to see that Caucasians do not have the market cornered when it comes to sports and PhD's and good ideas. Thinking bigger and pondering greater shows us the folly of prejudice and just why it is that exclusive can be an ugly word.

Thinking bigger and pondering greater can also engender humility. Many years ago a wealthy student at Williams College was accused of defacing college property and was sent to see President Mark Hopkins. He came in arrogantly, took out his wallet, and asked as to how much was the damages. This was too much for President Hopkins to take. He commanded the young man to sit down. "You can write me a check for the damages," so said the President, "but I'll have you know that no one, no one can pay for what it is he or she receives here. Can you pay for the sacrifices of Col. Williams who founded this college? Can you pay for the professors who remained here to teach when they could've gone elsewhere for a lot more money? Every student including you is a charity case. Every student including you has received far more than is deserved."

Life Injections IV

Thinking bigger and pondering greater will have us seeing the big picture and how we've been the recipient of the sacrifices of many people. How we've been a charity case ever since we were born and will be until the day we die. How we've been provided with advantages and opportunities far beyond what we deserve. Thinking bigger and pondering greater exposes our dependency, our debt to many people thus beating back the arrogance that doesn't recognize those truths.

And besides that, thinking bigger and pondering greater can be a source of consolation. I love that story of the cricket player whose dad was blind but still attended every one of his games. He would take delight in the comments he heard from the crowd in regards to the excellent play of his son. Then one day, the cricket player's dad died. The following Saturday, an important game was to be played. The other members of the team, who knew the player's affection for his blind father, took it for granted that he wouldn't be there. To their surprise, the young man came to the game. When the game began, he played like he had never played before. He was not only his usual excellent self but he played even beyond that excellence. He set records and, when the game ended, the crowd gave him a standing ovation. "You outdid yourself," said the coach, "how was it that you played so extraordinarily well, how was it that the grief from your dad's death didn't drag you down?" "Well," said the cricket player, "when I began the game, I realized that this is going to be the first game, the first time where my dad was going to be able to see me play."

By thinking bigger and pondering greater, we are able to discern that there's a life beyond this one, able to discern that there's more to life than this world in which we live. In so doing, we come to the realization that the promises of Christ are not as far-fetched as we might have once thought them to be. What that cricket player believed in regards to his once blind father is what Christ promised to those who love him and believe in him, a belief supported by bigger thinking and greater pondering.

And thinking bigger and pondering greater also calls for accountability. In his autobiography, the great preacher Harry Emerson Fosdick reminisced. "Many a time," he wrote, "many a time as I went to the pulpit I recalled a colleague Hugh Latimer whose pulpit happened to be in the Royal Chapel of Buckingham Palace. Heading to that Chapel one morning, Latimer heard a voice that said: 'Latimer, Latimer, be careful what you preach today because you are going to preach before the King of England.' But then he heard another voice that said: 'Latimer, Latimer be careful what you preach today because you are going to preach before the King of Kings and the Lord of Lords.'" So when Harry Emerson Fosdick entered the pulpit of the famed Riverside Church in New York City, he'd recall that Latimer anecdote and realize that God would be listening to his sermon and, that being so, he'd better be at his best and he'd better not to mince any words when it comes to the Gospel.

Thinking bigger and pondering greater has us recognizing that God is always on the premises. It has us hearing that second voice Latimer heard before he entered his pulpit. And with that comes our need to be on our best behavior. With that comes our need to live up to the high standards God has set for our life. And with that comes our need to ask ourselves as to whether God would sanction what it is we're doing. With that comes our need to think twice as to what we're about to do because God will be watching.

And then finally when it comes to thinking bigger and pondering greater, there is the esteem it happens to provide. Most of us are familiar with the Ash Wednesday charge: "Remember you are dust and to dust you shall return!" What we're usually not aware of, and what thinking bigger and pondering greater leads us to realize that the dust from which we're made and to which we shall return happens to be stardust. For, in fact, the dust of the earth is a result of an exploding star. And just as stars are beautiful and stars are awesome and stars are a wonder to behold, so therefore are we. God made us so and God told us so.

We're celebrating today what used to be called the feast of Corpus Christi or, as we call it today, the feast of the Body and the Blood of Christ. It's our annual reminder that we are a child of God, a brother or sister to Christ and, that being so, our family is huge. It encompasses the entire human race.

Corpus Christi has God doing what Michelangelo had done to Raphael's painting. It has God writing amplius across our minds and hearts. So my friends, think bigger and ponder greater. It can show you just how trivial are the worries and irritations that bother you. It can have you realizing as to how what you're doing is a vital part of a bigger whole, how your little job may be a part of the building of a cathedral. Think bigger and ponder greater and you'll see that despite your wealth, you're still a charity case and you'll see why the word exclusive is an ugly word.

Think bigger and ponder greater and you'll realize that you're being monitored by the King of Kings and Lord of Lords and you'll be consoled to know that in death your blind father can now see, your crippled mom can now walk, your Alzheimer's stricken grandfather can now think clearly. My friends, pay heed to that word amplius which God has written across your mind and heart. Make sure you focus on greater thoughts. Make sure you ponder greater things.

ENDNOTES

[1] Edgar Allen Poe, *Complete Tales and Poems* (Maplewood, NJ: Maplewood Books, 2013).

[2] Joshua Wolf Shenk, *Lincoln's Melancholy* (New York: Mariner Books, 2006).

[3] Margaret Mitchell, *Gone with the Wind* (NY: Macmillan Books, 1940).

[4] Hans Christian Anderson, *Fairy Tales of Hans Christian Anderson* (NY: Readers Digest, 2004).

[5] C.S. Lewis, *Screwtape Letters* (NY: Harper One, 2009).

[6] Malcolm Gladwell, *Outliers* (NY: Little Brown and Company, 2008).

[7] Frank Asch, *Good Lemonade* (NY: Scholastic library Publishing, 1976).

[8] C.S. Lewis, *Chronicles of Narnia* (NY: Harper Collins, 2001).

[9] Nathaniel Hawthorne, *The Birthmark* (Logan, Iowa: Perfection Learning, 2007).

[10] Chaim Potok, *The Chosen* (NY: Ballantine Books, 1996).

[11] Paul Pearsall, *The Beethoven Factor* (Charlottesville, VA: Hampton Road Publishers, 2003).

[12] Tom Brokaw, *The Greatest Generation* (NY: Random House, 2004).

[13] Gladwell, *Outliers*

[14] Alex Haley, *Roots* (NY: Gramercy Books, 2000).

[15] Antoine de Saint Exupéry, *The Little Prince* (NY: Harvest Publishing, 1971).

[16] In the final season, they were featured as villains who wished control of the world.

[17] Jean Giono, *The Man who Planted Hope and Grew Happiness* (White River Junction, VT: Chelsea Green Publishing Company, 1985).

18 Florence L. Barclay, *The Rosary* (NY: G.P. Putman & Son, 1911).

Richard E. Zajac

About the Author

Richard E. Zajac, known in many circles as "Fr. Duke" has been a staff chaplain at Sisters of Charity Hospital in Buffalo for the past 32 years. He is presently serving on many Boards and Committees throughout the community including Catholic Medical Partners, Town of Amherst Meals on Wheels, as well as the Perinatal Bereavement Network. He has chaired or co-chaired the Sister's Hospital Ethics Committee since its inception in 1984, and serves on the Ethics Committee for the Catholic Health Care System of Western New York. He's been an officer of the Parochial Baseball League since 1969 and was inducted into the Western New York Baseball Hall of Fame in 2007. He served on the National Advisory Council of the National Association of Catholic Bishops, and served as the Chairman of the Board of the Life Transition Center as well as the South Buffalo Community Development Association. He served on the Boards of the Upstate New York Transplant Services, Baker Victory Services, Bishop Timon High School as well as the American Cancer Society. He has also served 6 terms on the Priests' Council of the Diocese of Buffalo. He is the author of three books: *Life Injections I , II , III*.

www.ingramcontent.com/pod-product-compliance
Lightning Source LLC
Chambersburg PA
CBHW050312010526
44107CB00055B/2207